The Complete Manual
of
Catamaran Racing

The Complete Manual
of
Catamaran Racing

RICK WHITE

Illustrated

DODD, MEAD & COMPANY · NEW YORK

Library of Congress Cataloging in Publication Data

White, Rick.
  The complete manual of catamaran racing.

  Includes index.
  1. Catamarans. I. Title.
GV811.63.C3W47   797.1'4   76-10380
ISBN 0-396-07316-6

Contents

1. Getting Acquainted   1
2. The Big Sail   5
3. The Little Guy   29
4. Sticks   39
5. . . . and Stones   45
6. With the Wind Behind   51
7. Sports Car Steering   61
8. Bang!   66
9. Going Up!   78
10. Over the Hill   91
11. Care and Feeding   106
12. Watch It!   117
13. Whoops!   126
14. Bottoms Up   135
    Index   143

The Complete Manual
of
Catamaran Racing

~1~
Getting Acquainted

So you've bought a sailboat to go fast, and now you want one that goes faster. Perhaps your new boat is a shiny new Hobie 16, a Tornado, a Sol Cat, or some other of the many excellent catamarans to be found in the marketplace in this long-awaited "Age of the Catamaran." Perhaps you are trading up to a larger, more competitive boat, International or Olympic class. Or perhaps this boat is your very first multihull, or even your first sailboat.

In my opinion, whatever two or three hulls you sail, you have made exactly the right choice. In small boats (and perhaps in large ones too) it is infinitely more fun to go fast than slow. And it is infinitely more challenging to have to make the right decisions in half the time you'd have in a monohull boat, a much greater test of sailing judgment to deal with boats in which your competition can open up a 500-foot lead on you in seconds, far more athletically exhilarating to deal with a boat so sensitive to weight and its adjustment. Catamaran racing is wetter and wilder, and calls for more wisdom than monohull racing.

It is my hope in these pages to stimulate that wisdom that led you to select a catamaran in the first place, and suggest some analytical thinking that will lead you to get more performance out of your boat. The techniques and judgments we will discuss have grown out of my ten years of multihull racing—most of it successful, but with many setbacks and many instances when I was required to revise my thinking radically. You may well have to do the same, for, just as the techniques described here grew out of the evolution of the multihull, so tomorrow's techniques will be revisions to match the industry's continuing thrust for more performance and more pleasure.

It is often difficult to remember that the modern recreational multihull is a scant twenty-five years old, and, as a force in the marketplace, probably little more than ten. Monohull development has been going on for well over a hundred years. Many people within and without the boating establishment still regard the catamaran as a "cheater" boat, or no fit sailboat at all. While it is easy to put these critics in the category of those diehards who say, "If the Lord had wanted us to have fiberglass boats, He would have made fiberglass trees," you would do well to remember that many of the very early multihulls deserved the contempt heaped upon them—particularly in view of the wild claims made by their zealous developers and converts. Nearly all went to weather with only mediocre results. Often they were a real bitch to tack. And when you consider the ever present difficulty of righting after a capsize, you have to admit that many deserved what they got.

The honest, unbiased critic of today sees an entirely different boat. This is why we have a catamaran in the Olympics, and this is the story of that boat. The modern, ten-year-young catamaran will beat almost anything to the weather mark, it tacks easily, and present-day hardware leaves only folly or alcoholism as an excuse for a capsize. In bringing about this boating revolution in so short a time, the production and design men and women in catamarans have almost performed a miracle. Without such people as Rodney Marsh, Reg White, Hobie Alter, Rod MacAlpine-Downey, Carter Pyle, Gayle Heard, Rick Taylor, and Bob Kettenhoffen of North Sails, you and your twin-hulled vessel might still be the subjects of ridicule at your yacht harbor.

I recall some of the points in history when the ridicule stopped. The first year that Tornados were allowed as a class at CORK (the Canadian Olympic Training Regatta at Kingston), they were raced on the same course as the Solings. They never failed to lap the entire Soling fleet in the twelve-mile course, and completed each race of the series in under forty-five minutes. Few left that regatta with scorn for the Tornado. When Coast Catamaran sold over five thousand Hobie cats in little more than a year, few in the industry had any doubt that the catamaran was to be a force in the overall sailing scene. Fewer still in the world of yachting could, even grudgingly, deny that the designers of the boats and the sailors who sailed them had only begun to learn to tap the speed potential and the fun potential inherent in multihull concepts.

Each year has brought improvement in design, better sails, better hardware, and better sailors. From this collective experience, mixed with a healthy dose of good old "seat of the pants" sailing, I hope you will be able to take the helm and run with what we have learned so far—and I hope I will be running with you. Some things I can tell you point-blank; no ifs, ands, or buts. Some I can only allude to as probable cause, and only your own personal exploration will tell you if it fits you and your boat. Five years ago, a book such as this would have been obsolete within a week of its publication. Today I can assure you that what is coming in sailing techniques and hardware will be refinements of the basic developments chronicled in these pages.

One of the annoyances of my childhood was having to avoid and care for a young sapling my mother had planted in our yard, seemingly right in the logical path of any coaster wagon or bicycle. Now I drive past the house with a mixture of pride and mock parenthood, marveling at the beauty and strength of this great maple tree, a scant thirty years old.

The multihull has branched out, acquiring great strength, some beauty, and much to be proud of—and it too has been in the path of many a menacing coaster wagon. One wonders, in view of the immense accomplishment, what the next thirty years will bring to such an endlessly exciting sailing concept, especially now that it is big enough to take care of itself. Whatever happens, I hope this book will long be a viable basic primer and lead you to better and more enjoyable racing in this new catamaran age.

~~2~~

The Big Sail

It was once the case—and very apparently so—that the catamaran classes were completely dominated by the skipper who used the flattest mainsail and had a good tiller hand on a weather leg. He was the fellow who could start last and still be at that weather pin ahead of you with no sweat.

That notion has prevailed for some time and still prevails in some classes. Gradually, however, an evolution in sails and their shape has been taking place.

In the early days of the Shark class in the United States, the national races were always dominated by Dick McIlvray, Jr., of Charleston, South Carolina. Dick sailed with a very flat-cut main and used the maximum foot and hoist dimensions the rules would allow for that flat sail. If the rules specified a luff of twenty-seven feet, he had the sail cut at twenty-seven feet. His idea, I am sure, was to take advantage of all the canvas you were allowed, even at the expense of shape.

His winning pattern was to take this flat main and beat the pants off everyone else going to the weather mark. It is important to note that even though he was sailing with the most close-winded sails at any event and could point very high,

Dick would foot off a bit and run free. Though a competitor might outpoint him, Dick was imperturbable and just kept running free. Sure enough, he would be at the first pin in the number one spot.

When asked about reaching, downwind, or off-the-wind work, Dick would tell you that all the boats were so nearly the same on those points of sail that few positions would change—and, indeed, these legs were far more often than not a parade. Dick felt he could pretty well stave off the reaching competitor on the off-wind legs either by luffing him, covering him, or using some other tactical method—particularly since he was usually out front at the weather pin and had only to keep a challenger behind or under.

Even if he was passed—as he was a number of times—he still had more weather legs to work on that competitor. And with his ability to go upwind, he worried very little while off the wind.

This tactic lived a long time in the Shark class, and is still being used by a few of the top Shark skippers, but not nearly so effectively as in the days of McIlvray.

The next fad in the evolution of cat mains was the extremely full sail. North American Champion Betty Wells and her father, Bill Wells, using a very baggy and full-cut English sail, went on to dominate the class. They sailed holding on to what they could during the weather leg, and if they were even near the front of the pack at the weather pin, they were in great shape. After rounding the mark, that full sail would swoop past the flatter sails with little or no effort, even when a competitor with flat sails would try his tactics to the utmost. The superior downwind boat speed paid off. The full sail, as we all now recognize, is certainly the ticket sailing downhill, and the Wellses' bag sometimes looked more like a reaching spinnaker than a mainsail. It did a marvelous job.

From St. Petersburg, Florida, another skipper, Nick Stan, started using his full English sail to downwind advantage and added another trick to the bag of catamaran techniques. He started tacking downwind while the others were still playing with the old wing-and-wing procedure. Nick undid everyone after that, including another full-sail advocate, National Champion Jim LeCain, who tried a very full-cut North sail.

The full sail had become the mainsail of the era, as it not only had the ability to go off the wind well on any point of sail, but, with the innovation of tacking downwind, was even more demonstrably the superior cut in sails. Everybody stampeded to the nearest sailmaker to get a full-cut main.

The disadvantage of the full sail, of course, was its unsuitability for going to weather unless it was an extremely light-air day, there was a choppy sea, or the weight of the crew was heavy. Under those circumstances, it could be less of a disadvantage to have that fullness.

On a screaming beam reach and in just plain heavy air, the flat sail still was good off the wind, since all sails had more wind than they could use. The full sails did not scream by the flat ones on windy days, even downwind, and particularly not on close or beam reaches. And when it came to flat seas, the flat sail did very nicely on nearly all points of sail except downhill. So the advent of the full sail did not entirely knock out the flat; it was sort of a TKO with the full-cut dominating for the time being.

Then there was George Alleman, pioneer in the field of catamarans and chief gadgeteer for Reg White's Sailcraft, Ltd., of England. George had Gayle Heard of England sew him up a sail combining the best of all possible worlds into one beautiful sail. Its design was unique in the class and it quickly proved to be the universal sail that could go well to weather and, with a few minor adjustments that could be made quickly while under way, could also go like scat off the wind.

This sail was a flat sail, or it was a full sail, or it was medium sail (whatever medium is). It was whatever you wanted it to be: It could be adjusted to handle best the condition under which it was being sailed, be it beating, reaching, tacking downwind, or running.

Up near Ithaca, New York, Dr. Jack Carpenter sailed out on Lake Canandaigua with a computer-designed sail, similar in concept to Heard's sail. Carpenter shared the design with Jack Schuh of Miami, Florida, and they both found themselves back in the race for class domination. This new sail was in some ways different from its British counterpart, however. The Ithaca sail always performed far better in heavy air and seemed to lean toward flatness, while the English sail performed well in light to moderate wind and leaned toward fullness. My preference was for the British, for in addition to its fullness, it was undercut by at least six inches on the hoist and at least three inches on the foot. The Ithaca sail was nearly to maximum dimensions, thereby restricting its ability to stretch and change shapes easily. The English sail was of a soft material that played a large part in its ability to change shapes. The American sail was of conditioned, yarn-tempered Dacron, which is stiff, and it is somewhat difficult to alter.

Notice that the English sail was undercut and of soft material. It was a full sail, but, with the stretchiness available to it by virtue of the undercut and pliability, it could be made very flat as well. Its dimensions were less than maximum when set full for offwind or light air, and according to some theorists it lacked potential. However, in reality, it was able to set much better and was more easily adjusted than its American counterpart. In all probability, the sail may well have given you just as much canvas, but the flexibility afforded by the scant hoist and outhaul dimensions let you put it where it would do the most good.

The American sail, on the other hand, was a bit flat and could not be made full because of the lack of versatility that resulted from the material and size. Its ability to be adjusted was limited by its own features.

This was the "state of the art" when the Tornado came into its own in the sailing world. It brought with it a cluster of novel ideas, some radically new and some borrowed from monohull classes. Designed within the same sail-area parameters as the original Shark (International class B, 235 square feet), the Tornado was innovative in its use of a very tall mast and short boom. This very long luff permitted much greater reshaping with downhaul tensions. Equally important, the Tornado featured a loose foot, virtually terminating at the bottom batten, affording almost unlimited movement and control. The enormous roach that had been the hallmark of all early cats was nearly absent. With the sail, the Tornado ushered in a wild array of hardware for controlling its shape. Wheel-driven and geared downhauls permitted as much as two thousand pounds downhaul pressure on the luff. Mounted on a roller-bearing track, the geared outhaul had a movement of well over a foot. Here was a boat with a sail design that would allow it to go excellently to weather, and with a flick of a wrist (or maybe a couple of flicks of the wrist) it could turn around the weather pin and do wonders off the wind with its then full sail.

The gadgets the Tornado used were workable. This was a major breakthrough not only in sail design, but in the way to get the most out of that sail design. It is significant that nearly every new catamaran since the Tornado—notably the Hobie 16, Sol Cat, Unicorn, and Australis—has attempted to incorporate these innovative performance factors in their designs. Naturally, there were ideas used in the Tornado that could not be allowed by production requirements or class-rule considerations, but in general, most were quickly picked up.

The whole idea, of course, is to have a flat sail going to weather and in close reaches, and a very full sail while off the wind.

There are certainly many variances to that basic principle, dependent on crew weight, strength of the wind, wave action, and so on. But for the most part, it is an inviolable rule. Later we can get into the subjects of when to use what shape of sail and in what conditions, but now let's talk of how to get the sail in the shape required by the conditions.

Basic sail shape should be cut into your sail in the first place, as fighting shape can sometimes get you into a heap of trouble. But most good sails will adjust to a considerable degree. When having a sail cut, you should keep in mind such things as your normal crew weight, the prevailing conditions under which you sail, and—although this is a vague factor—how you yourself handle a boat. If you and your crew total up to the hefty side, you should probably be thinking of starting with a mainsail cut a little fuller than average. If you and the crew are featherweights, a flatter sail should do you nicely. However, whether you happen to be Porko von Popbottom or Lyndon Lightfoot, if you are sailing in choppy seas you could do very well to look for a full main.

In many North American classes you must buy your original or replacement sail directly from the factory or class-approved sailmaker. If you want to win, don't be too easily put off by the manufacturer's claim that all sails are identical. Try to go to the builder or sailmaker and select—or order—what will serve you best.

Keep in mind that when I say "full" or "flat," I am speaking relatively; we are still seeking the truly versatile sail.

In addition, the way you sail a boat is a determinant of sail selection. If you are one of those superhelmsmen who never misses a shift and stays right on it, you could get away with a relatively flat sail; a fuller sail will have the tendency to correct errors somewhat by its driving power. Don't let it scare you, but the maxim is: The flatter the sail, the more intense must be the concentration in order to get the benefit of its advantages.

Assume that you have a sail that is on the full side. There are a number of things you can do to flatten the sail; some should be done ashore, others can be adjusted afloat. One way to flatten a sail ashore is to use stiff battens. Some sailors have put double battens in each pocket to ensure stiffness, especially before a race in a real blow. By not tying the battens in tightly, you can also give the sail a flatter effect. The more tightly you tie in a batten, the fuller the sail should get. (This is not a hard and fast rule, as many production catamaran classes require specific factory standard battens that often can be so flexible that the reverse procedure is used in heavy air. The batten tension is *increased* to prevent the heavy airs and high speeds from reducing all sail shape to a sheet of plywood.)

Keep in mind that when you use the stiff batten and flatten your sail, that stiffness may be a big hindrance to your downwind speed. A leech line, running from the head to the clew, can be a big help if you are using stiff battens, as it forces camber (curvature) back into those stiffs. Generally, it will only force the camber in the top third of the sail and cannot be considered the entire answer to the desire for versatility.

Personally, I'd rather have a full sail, and not try to make it flat ashore. It's too irrevocable. I would much rather have the boat rigged to flatten the sail while afloat. That means the use of light battens of not more than three to six pounds of pressure. To measure the poundage of the batten, you can use an ordinary bathroom scale and a stepladder. Stand on the ladder and place one end of the batten on the scale and push down on the other end. When the batten has assumed its normal curvature, take a reading on the scale. If the scale reads fifteen, you're in trouble, in my opinion. When I sail, I prefer to have the battens near the four-pound mark or less. All of them should be fairly uniformly tapered as well. Foam-filled battens are presently being used that measure as low as three-quarters of a pound of pressure. However, most battens, both foam and wood, are now running between three and four pounds.

It is my view that the draft in your sail, if the sail is properly cut, should be approximately 30 percent aft, near the head, and should gradually work back to about 45 to 50 percent of the way as it nears the foot. The draft should be back farther near the bottom half of the sail to improve the slot complement with the jib, which will be operating primarily on the lower half of the main. The draft in the main should parallel the line formed by the leech of the jib. Start with that and then use downhaul, outhaul, and vang to move the center of effort back and forward as the point of sail may require.

The battens should be tapered with the main's draft in mind, so that they complement sail shape rather than fight it. Remember, shape should also be fairly uniform, panel to panel. Since battens deserve a great deal more attention than I can give them here, I have given them a chapter of their own later in the book.

Light battens in a full sail have always done well for me. I tie them in snugly—not too tight and not too loose. The tension on the batten should be just enough to lift the sailcloth horizontally. Rick Taylor of Taylor Made Sails in California (a highly creative sailmaker for catamarans) suggests the battens be bolted into place rather than tied. You can do this by passing a 10-32 stainless-steel bolt through the grommet and into a hole drilled in the batten. Taylor theorizes that this procedure gives you less flexion when you're in the process of filling or flattening your sail.

With the sail now on the mast and still full, we must use the boat to get the fullness out of the sail, assuming you prefer to get your sail flat by adjustments afloat rather than by using the land method of stiff battens. Another of the catamaran innovations for this purpose was again offered first by the Tornado—the bending mast. In bending the mast, you do not merely pull back on the top of it, but bow the midsection of the mast forward. If a plumb line were hung from the top of the mast, it could well look like Robin Hood's longbow. Inasmuch as you are pulling down on the leech, trying to make a straight line of it and thereby bending the mast like a bow, the sail (battens and all) moves into that arc formed by the bow. Consequence: a flatter sail.

To get the ultimate flatness, your sail must be outhauled and downhauled as far as possible. To aid in getting it that flat, and to draw the draft somewhat forward, you should have either a good downhaul with lots of purchase or a Cunningham hole—whichever your class allows—or both.

Think back on my comments about Dick McIlvray, whose sails were cut so as to get every square millimeter of sail area allowed by his class. If he had followed his theory, where would he be now? When he outhauled enough to flatten his sails, he would go past his maximum measurement bands on the boom. What would he do with the luff of his sail when he tried to downhaul enough to get the shape drawing in the right direction? It would be illegal if he tried to make his sail set properly, as he would exceed the mast measurement bands as well. Trying to get the sail to be versatile, he would be outlawed. A Cunningham might help him, but few catamaran classes allow them.

The sail must be undercut on the hoist and foot if it is to be stretched into the shape you want. A sail cut to the maximum specifications of the class with no consideration given to stretching and shaping is about as effective as having your boat Sanforized to avoid bow deflection when wet. Versatility is what we are after, and it can't be achieved by imprisoning your sails within maximum dimensions.

In some classes, there may be a real problem in bending the mast, but most masts bend more than the sailors who sail them realize. Study some of the many exciting Hobie regatta photos and you will see how much this stick—one that we think of as being heavy and unyielding—really bends, "esses," and changes sail shape in the process. The Tornado was designed from the beginning to have a mast that bends, but what of the others? Sharks never bent their masts until 1971, when I arrived in Florida for the Coconut Grove Sailing Club's Annual Shark Midwinter Nationals with a definite game plan along this line.

I had been sailing my Tornado for only a short while, but

waste

I had learned a few tricks that could easily be transferred to the Shark. One of these was playing with the diamond stays. The stays are a determining factor in the flexibility of a mast. If you took them off, the mast would bend plenty; as a matter of fact, it would break. But putting a lot of slack in them will allow the mast to bend, but not to the breaking point. If the diamonds are very tight, the mast will bend very little, whereas if they are loose, the mast will bend considerably.

Another factor is the mast rotation, which goes hand in hand with the diamonds. The more the mast rotates, the more the sail pulls on it from the side and the more it will bend. Most contemporary cat masts, being tear-drop or oval in profile, resist bending fore and aft, but when turned will allow considerably more flexibility. So for the Shark regatta, I promptly removed my standard mast rotation stoppers and installed an adjustable gooseneck mast rotation controller. Next was the installation of an adjustable outhaul mounted on the end of the boom. That was a simple task, as there are many variations of outhauls on the market.

Loaded with all these ideas and equipment, I charged out into Biscayne Bay to see what would happen in competition.

The wind was fresh and the seas were not as sloppy as those to which I was accustomed, and so I considered them smooth. Others might have disagreed, but I wanted to see how my ultraflattener would work. Dr. Jack Carpenter blew his mast in one of the early races and everybody behind me thought I would be next. It was the first time they had ever seen a Shark mast pushed so hard. I did not break the stick, but rather just sizzled up the weather legs. And I had made no sacrifices in downwind ability, either, and easily took the regatta.

Later I tried to pump Dr. Carpenter to see if he had been

experimenting with the mast bend, too (which I strongly suspected). He immediately offered me a Manhattan and
changed the subject.

Mast rotation plays a big part in the amount of mast bend
that can be accomplished in either the Shark or the Tornado.
The more the mast is rotated, the more it is able to bend.
The more it is able to bend, the flatter the sail will become.
If conditions call for a bit fuller sail going to the weather pin
(choppy seas, light airs), you need not rotate the mast so
much and the stick will not bend as much—and your sail will
not be quite so flat. To flatten the sail: outhaul, downhaul,
fully rotate the mast, and honk on the mainsheet.

A bonus to the full-rotated mast in some designs is the
ability to get the jib closer hauled. For when the mast is fully
rotated, the spreader will be farther forward and will allow
the leech of the jib to come closer to the mast. You should be
careful, however, to keep a productive relationship between
the jib and the main. Backwinding your main with your jib
will certainly not add to your boat speed.

If you do not already have an adjustable mast rotation
stop, they are very easy to install on nearly all boats. Be sure
to check your class rules first, to be certain you are not making some outlawed modification that may be costly to rectify.

On the early Sharks, the mast step and combined rotator
was cast with stops at about 45 degrees on either side, more
or less. Many small cats still have the same sort of arrange-
ment. What I did was to cut off the mast rotation stoppers
that were built in. You will probably find you can do the
same on your boat. Now you have nothing at all to prevent
the mast from rotating, and you can go on to a controller—
and you must!

For the controller, acquire some good, strong tubing of at

least one-half-inch diameter and approximately two feet in length. Cut it in half, flatten the ends, and drill holes through each end. Bolt the two ends together so the tubing is parallel and drill another hole closer to the end. This is where you will want to put a shackle to which you will attach a line, and that line will lead directly to the underside of your boom. There you can install a jam cleat. After that, take the free ends and spread them apart, bending them wide enough so that each will go on either side of the mast. It should look very much like a wishbone. Attach it to the mast midway on each side by a bolt that goes all the way through the spar. It should be mounted no lower than six inches below the lowest point of the boom. If it is too low, the wishbone will be cocking up too high and will allow the mast to go nearly all the way around. That could prove to be a disaster. If it is too high, it may get jammed up into the boom itself.

Still a better way is to buy a ready-made wishbone from a specialist in catamaran parts; most of them have a device of this nature. Keep in mind that there is a lot of pressure exerted on this wishbone once it has rotated past the 40-degree mark. The more rotation, the more pressure. Things will also have a greater tendency to break when overrotating. And the next time you are winning a regatta and have only to go out and stay near an opponent, don't push such "go fasts" as overrotation to the hilt, for a breakdown may put you out of the regatta.

To ensure that the wishbone does not bend under pressure, you might weld a flat plate between the legs of the wishbone, about halfway down it. This additional gusset should make the controller virtually indestructible.

Now that we have more or less made a flat sail out of your

rather full one, let us try to make it full again. In part, it is simply a matter of releasing what you have used to get it flat. But I suggest you do even more.

You may now ease the outhaul of your main. This will help to make the bottom of the sail relatively full, but will offer very little assistance to the top of the sail. When you are striving for fullness, of course, you will not be sheeting the main very tightly, and this will ease the leech and help things aloft. Leech lines will aid in getting the top of the sail fuller, but will be of very little help near the bottom. By using the combination of the two, inhauling and hardening up the leech line, you can balloon the sail very well.

For some, the leech line works very nicely along with the inhaul, but combine those with the boom vang and you are a real threat to the competition sailing downwind. Since the leech wire is connected to the outhaul traveler car (or should be, if it isn't) without a boom vang, the tightened wire simply lifts up the boom and your leech line effect ends up at best a nominal advantage. With the vang keeping the boom down, the leech line really applies maximum tension to the battens and pushes them toward the mast (more easily done if you are sporting lightweight battens and need only four pounds of pressure to bend them), bellying out the main. If you have a good boom vang, you can now leave the main-sheet traveler at dead center. That should make jibes much easier and quicker. Otherwise you must run the car to the very end of the traveler track and then sheet fairly hard. This has the further disadvantage of pulling the boom a bit back inboard, which will not help your ability to point deep in downwind tacking.

Mast rotation as a device to increase mast bend is not a factor going downhill. Still, you want it to rotate as far as possible to create a maximum pocket. It's almost impossible to overrotate, as the shrouds will prevent it. Since you're not honked down on the boom and it is taking almost the same angle as the mast, there is no bend.

So, off the wind, put fullness in your main by inhauling, easing the mainsheet, use of the leech line, and maximum mast rotation, and you have gained the versatility needed to get the ultimate from your boat.

Now that we've discussed the relatively full sail, let's talk about the flat sail that needs adjustment in order to make it fuller.

For adjustments ashore, the placement of stiff battens would defeat your purpose of getting the sail fuller, so the choice should be light battens—probably lighter than those you used in the fuller sail. To gain a bit of extra fullness with adjustments ashore, tie the battens in very tightly. Getting them to change their camber from one tack to another may be difficult, but at least you have done something about getting fullness in the sail.

Whenever battens are tied in tightly, they have a bad habit of wanting to poke through the luff of the sail. There is nothing more disheartening than looking up the sail in the heat of battle to see a batten poised like an arrow through the sail and past the mast. A good preventative is to drill a small hole through the sail, batten and all, near the luff and before the boat rope (this area is built up by the sailmaker, usually with double material, webbing, or plastic), and stick in a small-diameter stainless-steel nut and bolt with large washers on either side. Tighten the hell out of them!

With the sail mounted, you should have no problem flattening it, for it wants to seek its natural level. If you suddenly find yourself wanting to make it still flatter, then you can apply the measures we discussed before.

But the problem with this sail is increasing its fullness. On the water, the reverse order is therefore indicated. Since this sail is already flat, we do not want much mast bend, if any at all. Mast bend will flatten out what sail fullness we have. Accordingly, the diamond stays should be as tight as possible to reduce mast bend. The mast rotation controller should be set more tightly than with the full sail. It should not be set too much in line, however, or there will be a bad effect on the leading edge of the mast which will ruin the sail's efficiency.

Inhauling, and perhaps even a leech line, could be instrumental in increasing the fullness of the sail. The problem with the leech line when beating, or any excessive leech controls, is that sometimes the leech tends to be hooked to weather and acts as a windbrake. I would rather see the leech fall off a little. The leech line is very good off the wind, for a hook in the sail can be a blessing on that point of sail.

In 1970 at the Norfolk, Virginia, Shark Nationals, Stan Woodruff and I tied for first place—much to my chagrin. With the sweet savor of revenge on my lips, I showed up at North Star Yacht Club on Lake St. Clair, Michigan, to race him again in his own water only a few weeks later. The course was once around a huge triangle. We were racing among a bunch of auxiliaries with masts as high as the Sears building. The first two legs of the course I can describe only in four-letter words, for the wind was fluky and what there was of it was scarfed up by those big bummers. But, be that as it may, the wind picked up to moderate, with a typical Lake St. Clair chop (mostly stinkpotter-generated). Stan rounded the last mark four boat lengths before me and headed for the finish line, some three miles away, on a beam reach. Marks had been to starboard, so obviously we had just come off a downwind tacking situation. My leech wire was still set and outhaul fully slacked. As we rounded the last mark, I gave chase, heading just a bit high temporarily to stay out of Stan's sail wash. (In cats, the shadow and backwind are thrown far back—effectively much farther than in a monohull.) From that position, Stan and I stayed at identical speeds in identical wind and wave conditions. Even our crew weights were close to the same.

My thinking at the time was that because of the chop, the leech line should be on so that the sail would stay full and we would keep our driving power. But since I was not passing him, I was certainly not content with the situation. After a few hundred more yards and with the finish line looming only a couple of miles ahead, I reached up and released the line.

That did the trick, for soon we chomped right over the top of him, being careful not to get down too close lest he run us up. Obviously the leech line had been too much of a hook and was acting as a brake. We needed the fullness, but we didn't need the brake on at the same time.

This was an obvious advantage of a naturally full sail. For, by artificially filling it, the leech line had brought about adverse effects. I still do not know if Stan had his leech wire on at the time or not, but I suspect he did, giving us the advantage of a full sail and a leech that straightened out the air, not stopped it. We went on to win the race by a considerable margin.

If the contemporary sail is going to be successfully campaigned downwind, the mast must be stiff, the outhaul eased forward as far as it can go, the leech line really honked down, the traveler out as far as possible, and enough tension on the mainsheet to hold the boom in a low enough position for the leech line to be effective. If you are sailing a boat without a leech line, reason will tell you that mainsheet tensions must be carefully set in order not to pull the leech aloft down flat. With all that, the sail should become fairly full.

For reaching, the same items must be tended, but in moderation. Yet if the sail was very flat in the first place, even a beam reach may require extreme adjustments for best performance.

Let's review the flat sail: It needs very little doctoring to gain flatness, as that is built into it. Should further flatness be desired, remember that outhauling, downhauling, diamond-slacking with full mast rotation, and hard sheeting will flatten a sail. Any one of these items or all of them will do something toward flatness, and a bit of figuring where the fullness is will tell which remedy to take first.

To make a full sail, employ inhauling, diamond-tightening, lessened mast rotation, and moderate sheeting. If the sail has been cut very flat, you may need to use not just one of these measures, but all of them.

At this point we should have gained a great deal of versatility in our sail, which is needed to exact the ultimate performance from our catamaran. The concepts of getting the sail flat, full, or whatever are now with us. But when we should use each is a matter of tremendous import.

Sailors must be able to apply the proper tool to the proper problem. Various conditions will demand a certain setting of the sail—a setting that unfortunately cannot be determined by mathematics, but we can try to evolve a formula nonetheless. Experience is undoubtedly an excellent teacher, but perhaps we can create a rule of thumb by which to judge.

There are three prime factors that help you judge how your sails should be adjusted. Let's call them "the three Ws."

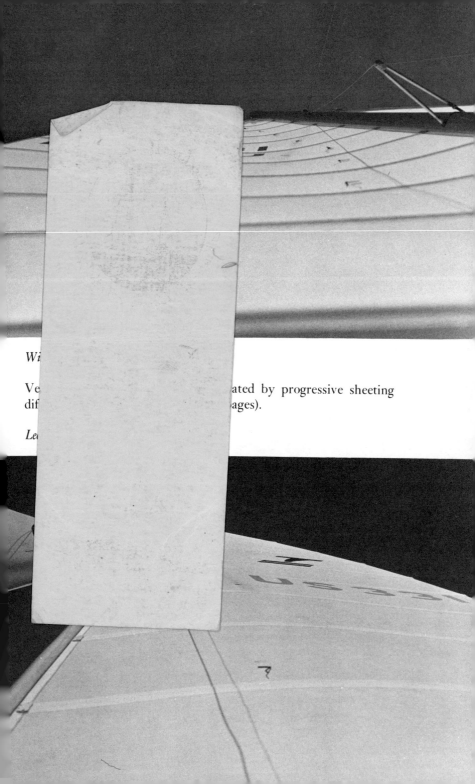

Wi

Ve   ated by progressive sheeting
dif   ages).

Le

Windward setting with little sheeting.

Leeward setting with little sheeting.

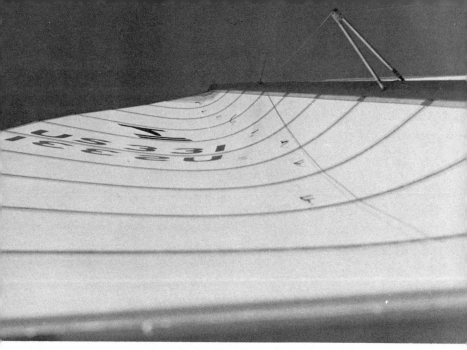

Windward setting with moderate sheeting.

Windward setting with moderate sheeting.

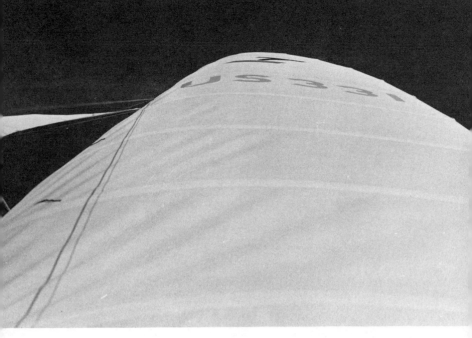

Leeward setting with downhaul and outhaul eased, and moderate sheeting.

They are Wind Conditions, Wave Conditions, and Weight Conditions aboard.

It should go without saying that lighter air requires a fuller sail, while heavier air requires a flatter sail; that heavier seas require a fuller sail while calmer seas require a flatter sail; that heavier crew weight requires a fuller sail while lighter crew weight requires a flatter sail.

Take Boat A, which has a lightweight crew aboard (requiring a flat sail) and is sailing in light air (requiring a full sail) in a choppy sea (requiring a full sail). How should the sail be set? Full? Moderate? Flat? My answer would be that the skipper needs a pretty full sail with a slight moderation toward flatness. In two Ws out of three, this boat needs a full sail. The majority wins; it's the democratic way! The sail need not be set to its fullest, however, as the crew's light weight allows for a bit of flatness.

Boat B has a moderate-weight crew (moderate) and is sailing in heavy air (flat) and flat seas (flat). Two Ws out of three say a flat sail, but with moderation toward a medium sail because of the crew weight. If the crew had been lightweight, an extremely flat sail could be used.

Alongside another boat, or in race conditions where you have a ready measure of boat speed, you have the perfect opportunity to find the perfect "moderate" for your machine. Since you can easily figure the moderate intermediate starting point, try pulling the strings slightly, one at a time, to see how best to adjust for maximum boat speed.

Boat C, with a heavy crew (full), is sailing in light air (full) and in choppy seas (full). Three of the three Ws dictate a full sail. This boat will need it, too, and will still probably stand little chance against its lighter competitors.

The point is to analyze the three Ws of weight of crew, wind conditions, and wave conditions, and determine what you need to apply in a particular case as it arises. In the course of a race, conditions may vary a great deal, and you must vary with them.

Basically, this scheme is applicable only in going to weather. For it is my contention that there is no room at all for a flat sail downwind, no matter what the crew weight (even though a lightweight crew can get by with less drive downwind than a heavier crew can), no matter what wave action may exist (although a flatter sail will not be hurt as badly in a calm sea), and no matter what the wind velocity is (even though in a blow the flat sail will not be hurt to the degree it would be in light air).

It's a fact that I personally have sailed downwind with a flat sail, but that was in survival conditions with a good leg lead and I was too frightened to worry about a full or flat sail. I am equally sure my next competitor was not very worried about it either.

The rule for downwind, then, is quite simple: Sail with a full main no matter what the conditions. I use a leech line or anything else I can get my hands on to make the main a full one. The wing-and-wing theory of making a big barn door may be fine for some, but when you make a near-reaching spinnaker out of the main, you will have a mover.

A close reach can be treated very much as a beat, for the sailing characteristics and handling of the boat are very similar to those used in a beat. Perhaps the easing of the sheets, giving a little more fullness, allows for a little more drive. On the beam reaches, since the apparent wind moves so far forward with a catamaran, it is preferable to leave things pretty much the same as on a close reach, although you are going to need a bit more fullness. You will hardly ever be able to use a leech line on a beam reach, for it usually hooks the leech of the main, putting on the brakes. The apparent wind is just too far forward for hooking the main on the screaming reaches.

For reaches, then (except close reaches), you may use the above as a rule of thumb. Figure the three Ws and add another automatic factor of fullness and you should just about have it. By that standard, for our earlier Boat A—light crew (flat), light air (full), and choppy seas (full)—add another factor for full and you have three out of four that dictate a full sail, and full speed ahead!

--3--
The Little Guy

Despite the main's full-battened configuration, outhauls, downhauls, and so on, the jib is by far the more adjustable sail of the two. A catamaran requires battens in a main basically to hold the sail shape that the high, forward-moving apparent wind would knock out of a monohull sail if the boat could go that fast. Most jibs, on the other hand, have only small battens in the leech, if that, and since they are merely flexible cloth, they are far more subject to adjustment. Catamarans such as the Hobie 16 have full-battened jibs. The battens in this case function to hold shape in the jib despite a sheet lead angle that would otherwise distort the sail. If you have such a jib, a little experimentation with lead and batten tension will show you that this jib too is extremely adjustable, though much of the adjustment cannot be carried out under way.

The jib is probably the most important sail on most catamaran one-design boats. In most catamarans that I have sailed, it has been *the sail* to be concerned about. With the jib properly set and the boat properly sailed, the cat will move; set wrong, the jib will drain the power of the main, and the boat can't get out of its own way. The jib is responsible for

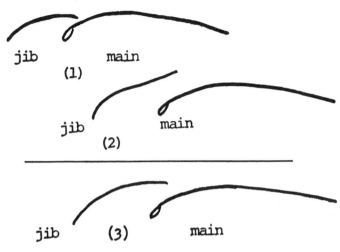

Slot is the all-important consideration in trim. Position (1) shows a jib over-sheeted choking off the slot and backwinding the main. In (2) the jib is under-trimmed. If this were a Tornado jib, the leach would be flopping but trim like this can easily go unnoticed in battened jibs such as a Hobie or Sol Cat. (3) is just right. Though the foot looks to be too close and backwinding, the bulk of the sail would undoubtedly be perfect in its relation to the main.

giving the boat pointing ability for weather work, yet is equally a contributor to good downwind sailing. However, there is still another sail behind the jib, and it is not to be ignored; after all, it's many times bigger. When I say the jib must be set properly, it is with regard to the main. In other words, the jib is *the sail* because it can multiply the power and efficiency of the main.

If you have a well-shaped, driving main and a jib set to complement it, then you really have a winner.

My ideas on the setting of the jib leads are by no means new or exciting. I simply try to set jib leads so that the leech shape from the top of the sail to the clew creates a slot parallel to the line created at that point by the line of the mainsail.

Back when I was making my first experiments in cats, sailing in Biscayne Bay at the 1968 Midwinter Multihulls being held at Coral Reef Yacht Club, I had some jib lead travelers on my trampoline but really did not know what to do with them. So I more or less set them any old place that seemed neat and let it go at that. In those early days of multihulls, not many were eager to sail cats and my sixty-year-old mother was my crew. The two of us struggled away to a near-last-place finish.

Between races we bobbed around in the bay, waiting for the second race (which was supposed to have been back to back with the first), and after two hours I noted that the boat seemed to move faster with the leads set farther aft when going to weather. Unfortunately, at the time I didn't know why. The next race finally started, and with the leads set aft, we took off like a big blue bird. No, we did not win. But I suppose that was due to my poor tactics. At the time, it taught me something; I just didn't know it until much later.

Years after, I noticed that when the leads were set aft going to weather, they pulled the foot of the sail aft, thereby letting the leech fall off a bit and take to the contour of the sail shape of the main. Conversely, when I left the jib leads forward, the lead pulled down and cupped the leech of the jib, making it tight and tending to hook the flow of air back into the main.

By all appearances, the jib did not seem to be backwinding the main, but the boat simply did not move.

With this information I tried setting up a roller-bearing traveler on my Shark, which moved diagonally from forward and outboard to aft and inboard. In this manner I could run my jib leads forward and outboard or aft and inboard. I knew I needed them inboard and aft when beating, and I knew I wanted them outboard and forward when reaching or running, thus creating a fuller sail and allowing a bigger slot between the jib and the main.

It took a few races to find the exact spots for the setting of the jib leads, but once they were found, the boat really moved. It seems odd, and it contradicts everything everyone has written or said, but that boat moved best when it had a little leech flutter while going to weather, particularly in decent air. The apparent reason for this is that in letting the jib leech fall off, you are beginning to twist off the head of the sail slightly and allowing the leech of the sail to match the contour of the main, producing a reduction in backwinding of the main, and allowing a better flow across the luff and lee side of the big sail.

Take your sturdy craft out for a sail in various wind conditions. Have someone handle the helm while you go down on the leeward side to check the contour of the sails. With your hand grab the jib lead and set it where it best allows the leech of the jib to follow the lines of the main all the way down, particularly near the bottom third of the sail. Now sail it on a reach and do the same thing, again holding the sail's lead so that it best follows the contours of the main. Next try a position midway between the extremes. After finding the spots you want, figure out a way to set the jib leads to maintain these relative shapes.

Remember, you were looking for a near parallel line to the shape of your main through the entire length of the jib leech, both in going to weather and off the wind. Don't be afraid of extreme inboard jib lead settings, either, for they will probably let the major portions of the leech fall off to match your main.

A problem that may arise with this type of jib lead setting is that the sheet trim may be very sensitive. The reason for the sensitivity is simply that a few millimeters of tension or slack on the foot results in inches on the leech. The virtue is that the boat speed will be tremendously increased and pointing ability will be much improved if the sail is properly trimmed. With the inboard setting, the curve of the jib leech will be paralleling the sail shape on the mainsail. When one click too many on the ratchet block occurs, you will be badly overtrimmed, closing the slot dramatically and badly backwinding the main. So next you ease it. Ease it too much and you will have lost most of the pointing ability, for you will have lost too much power in the upper part of the jib. With this type of jib setting you really want it just right.

If your class rules allow it, you may wish to install any one of a number of devices for jib lead settings. A traveler track works really well, but perhaps best when you have a solid tramp. In my Shark I used lightweight roller-bearing track, which could be sent flying forward and outboard by a flick of the wrist, or set up aft and inboard for beating to weather by a solid tug.

Since the Shark has wooden trampoline decks, it was easily installed, but fabric trampolined boats have another problem. In the past the way to set leads on fabric trampoline-type boats had been with a cable harness system that was strung across the deck and trampoline (which are terribly hard on the shin skin) or a mass of lines entangled like spider webbing called "barber haulers."

Far more fitting to a trampoline-type boat is a plastic-covered cable from the rear beam to the forward beam and secured inboard or outboard, anywhere on the beam that you want. This makes an ideal lightweight traveler. To operate the traveler, mount a roller block on the cable before final in-

The "West Coast System," inboard and outboard barber haulers with inboard leads through bottom of the boom. Mast rotation controller is above downhaul and tied in with outhaul. Many top racers are now abandoning this complex system.

stallation, which can be attached to a sheet block. From the roller block an adjusting line should run aft through a roller at the after end of the cable and to a cleat. Properly engineered, this idea should be even better than a traveler track.

Something to remember here in setting the jib lead traveler for downwind work: You have a crew that can hold the lead of the sail in all weather but a blow, so extreme forward setting may not be necessary. Usually even in extreme weather conditions the crew is the best barber hauler aboard downwind. In anything but a full gale, the jib should be hand-held on nearly everything past a beam reach.

Another jib lead idea is to have the traveler attached to the inboard gunwale of the boat, running from the forward to the after beam, to which your jib lead can be attached. Then from the boom set up an adjustable inhauling line that can adjust the sheets inboard, bringing the clew inboard.

The inhauling device on the boom itself should be a fairlead located between one and three feet aft of the mast, and a cleat another foot to a foot and a half behind that. The line to be used should have either a ring or pulleys that are attached to the sheet between the clew of the sail and the jib lead block on both port and starboard sides. The lines should come through the fairlead and combine into a single line and lead aft to the cleat.

By hardening up on the inhaul you will be pulling in on the sheets evenly on both tacks, and in consequence will be preset for either tack. Also, you will have the inhaul ability to set the clew of the jib anywhere between the inside gunwale of the boat all the way to the boom. The forward and aft settings can be controlled by the traveler track located on the inside gunwale. For additional forward and aft settings, the boom fairlead may be mounted on a traveler track also.

The inboard/outboard setting is determined to a large extent by boom position, which is supposed to be a big advantage according to the proponents of this system.

Sheeting will be very tender. The sheet should be set so that the jib is almost touching the spreader tip on the mast. To get the maximum drive from the jib and not backwind the main, you could have a slight amount of jib leech flutter.

You will be trimming quite differently for various wind conditions. This corresponds to the versatility you have in your main. Should the air be fairly good and the sea flat, you know that you can flatten the main and jib, close the slot somewhat, and be able to point much better. To flatten the main, you may overrotate the mast, and sheet very hard. With the main flatter there is less chance of backwinding by the jib, except that the more you have to bend the mast to flatten the main, the more chance you have of bowing the mast forward and into the slot. Generally, you may be able to sheet the jib tighter with the flat main. With the mast overrotated, you will also be able to bring the jib in very tight and still not backwind the main.

If conditions require a fuller setting of the main, the jib sheet should be eased to maintain its relative position with the contour of the main.

If all of the foregoing is too much for you, or if you feel you are getting in trouble, let me remind you that the man who has the second best investment in your performance is your sailmaker. If he is close, get him down for a sail and have him help you with the lead problem. If he is far away, ask him to send you a diagram of the layout that he has found to be the best companion for his jibs on your type of boat. But remember, his suggestions are not infallible. Experiment!

A very necessary adjustment on the jib is the luff control, easing or tightening the leading edge of the jib. By tightening the luff, you are stretching it. The stretch makes a reduction in the sail draft, and moves the sail draft forward toward the luff. Conversely, by easing the luff of the jib, you will be filling the sail and moving the draft aft.

Obviously, in going to weather, where the apparent wind wants to keep forcing the draft of the sail aft, you want to keep the draft forward as much as possible. The more the wind, the farther aft it will blow the draft, and the more you need to force it forward, or the more you need to tighten the luff control. By tightening the luff, you are also flattening the sail to offset the increased fullness being blown in, and particularly flattening the leech of the sail. And don't forget that this increased flatness allows you to point a degree or two closer to the wind.

There is a direct relationship between the luff tension and the amount of air blowing on the sail, as well as the direction from which it is blowing. As the air lightens, so must the luff tension in order to maintain a fuller, more driving sail.

Off the wind, with most properly cut jibs, there should be practically no tension on the luff; if any, just enough to keep the wrinkles out of the luff.

Luff devices can be either a halyard type or a downhaul type, or some variant of the Cunningham hole. Some have argued against the jib luff downhaul because in lowering the luff in order to gain tension, you lower the entire lower portion of the sail. You not only are lowering the luff of the sail, you are also lowering the clew. If you are using standard set positions for the jib lead, this may throw off the jib lead settings considerably. Others, however, argue that the lower positions are more to be desired.

The halyard-type luff tensioner allows the sail to be set at its lowest point at all times and should not affect the lead positions. With this system, when you tighten the luff, there are supposedly no adverse effects on the balance of the system.

The virtue, if only nominal, of the downhaul tensioner is that it is faster and easier to operate than the others. In the tide of battle, speed in setting your sails is essential. Some sailors believe that luff tensions should be changed many times on one weather leg, if variations in gusts change anywhere over a few knots. That could well be stretching things too far, yet it does stress the point that luff adjustments are essential.

One good luff tensioner, based on the downhaul theory, is

a cable run from either forward beam. At its attachment point on each beam there should be a cleat for both sides, and a three-to-one purchase to the cable. The cable then should run through the pulleys located on the boat at the attachment points of the forestay bridle. From there the cable should come up to the jib tack attachment point and be attached in such a way that it will downhaul your jib. With this setup you can quickly adjust the luff tension of the jib from either side of the boat with a three-to-one purchase.

Whatever you do, adjust and adjust, until it becomes automatic to set your jib to create a perfectly matching slot to the back side of the main. And as you adjust, keep checking, checking, checking. On your jib-handling ability may well rest your catamaran racing success.

~4~

Sticks

Weight aloft makes boats tippy. Catamaran sailors fear capsize, yet sail around with a small lumberyard aloft. The average monomaran sailor might deem us batty, sailing around in a boat with extra weight anchored up in its sails, as we do with our battens. Many think the only reason for the full-battened main is to support the extreme roaches that were characteristic of all the early catamarans. However, a little thought should reveal their major function. Since multi-hulls approach and even exceed the speed of the wind, without those battens in the sail, those speeds could not be maintained because the sail would collapse. So the batten weight was accepted as necessary, and a lot of thinking and planning has been put into improving battens and their effects on the mainsail.

My first battens were untapered ash, the lightest and best batten to be found back in those days. They did create some problems at most regattas, for inevitably a few battens would be broken, thereby ruining your beautifully matched set.

Then came innovation, and fiberglass, plastic, aluminum, et al. were experimented with. Most of them were discarded, but some continued on. I acquired a set of battens that were breakproof. With the breakproof battens, I could attend the weekend regatta and rest assured that my battens would survive. They were tapered ash, laminated with fiberglass. Rejects from the senior pole-vaulting and track team, they were so stiff it was all I could do to bend them. You can imagine the results after they were mounted in my sail. It gave me a lot of opportunity to inspect the wake action from assorted boats and a thorough examination of a good number of transoms.

Back to ash and the drawing board. The experience in stiff battens convinced me that the secret had to be a lighter batten, not so stiff. The ash, even though not tapered, did a far better job, because it was less stiff.

There are definitely times when a stiff batten is desirable, however, and this is not a total condemnation of them. For example, in heavy air and sea, most catamarans do best when footing off and driving through the waves. If at this time you are wearing lighter battens, you may find your sail is too full and is creating quite a heeling force. The boat may be nearly impossible to hold down. While it is true that the fullness will aid in driving through the waves, the excess heeling forces are causing a loss of power for you. Therefore, it is best to use either stiff battens, or those with moderate tensions, in the top of the sail (where the heeling force is created) and somewhat normal battens on the lower part of the sail (maintaining your power). The stiff battens at the top create less drag and less power, but also less heeling moment. Stiff or moderately tensioned battens will allow the top of the mainsail to twist off more easily, putting the power down low.

For general conditions, however, the lighter battens are able to do more for you.

Luckily for all of us, fiberglass arrived. George Alleman was the first to experiment with fiberglass battens, and began by making a few sets for his friends. It looked like the average batten, untapered, approximately two inches wide and three-sixteenths of an inch thick, but with a rib running right down the middle on each side. The rib determines the stiffness of the batten. By shaving off the rib in the first 30 percent or 40 percent of the batten, you can effectively taper it. It became a simple thing then to get the blanks and taper the battens to your own concepts, with the draft either forward, aft, or somewhere in between.

When tapering of this innovation began, along with it came success. The battens became extremely versatile, and so sail lofts began making sails that were more versatile too. With this new batten, one could flatten the sail to weather and make it full downwind. In reality, this concept recognized the ability of the sailcloth—not the batten—to respond to different wind conditions and points of sail. The earlier sail design would either get you to the weather pin first or have you swooping downwind swiftly, but few boats could do both.

There were problems, though. After you got your perfect set of fiberglass battens that were unbreakable, that were adjustable, that were fairly light, that would not rot, and that won some races for you, you began to notice that something was going wrong. Gradually through the season the boat lost its spark, its drive, began sailing the way it did back when. The culprits were the battens. The older the fiberglass, the stiffer it got. The stiffer it got, the worse the boat sailed.

All of this substantiated my belief that a lighter batten, one not so stiff, did a lot better job in almost all conditions.

It was back to the drawing board again. Apparently glass

was the answer to a lot of batten problems, and so Alleman and others began creating a much smaller, lighter batten, which is probably a little too light in the beginning but develops into the perfect batten as it ages.

Meanwhile, the rejected pole-vaulting idea had been rejuvenated by Gary Seaman of California. The Seaman batten was of tapered wood laminated with fiberglass and phenolics, similar to the ones I'd used before, but with an improved technique. Seaman's battens became extremely popular among the West Coast sailors in many classes, and rightly so, for the shape was well tapered and the battens were nice, bendy, and lightweight. They were tapered at the time of manufacture and could not be altered, however. The taper was built into them as a matter of standard procedure, with no alterations possible. The fiberglass batten was heavier and somewhat stiffer, but could be tapered by the boat owner to his specifications and needs.

Another batten made of tubular plastic was introduced. To taper these, you must shave along the sides of the tube, narrowing its sidewall resistance, and thereby allowing more flexion to occur.

One of the most recent developments on the market, and one met with a great deal of indecision, is a batten of foam plastic laminate, much the same as the Seaman wood batten. Some anticipate a problem here, since there is no tapering at all and the sailcloth must handle the entire duty of placement and amount of draft. The batten is very light in weight, and also very light in pressure resistance (independent of the sailcloth), which could be a very good thing. Advocates of this batten claim that the weight of both the sail and the battens does not add up to the weight of other battens alone. Obviously, reducing weight aloft is a great idea. Those questioning the modern versions of battens wonder if the inherent limited strength that allows them to be preshaped may not prevent them from producing the effect that a batten should give.

On the other hand, it is impossible that proper tensions on modern sailcloth may effectively work without the aid of tapering.

At any rate, batten production has come a long way, hand in hand with the inventive sailmakers who have worked to produce the ultimate in versatile sails. Now, with the advent of improved wood-processed battens, fiberglass battens, and foam-laminated battens, when going to weather you can possibly have a nice flat weather sail, and when rounding that pin, let it all hang out for a sizzling downhill ride.

Hobie Alter, himself, started the revolution that made cats truly popular and a part of the yachting scene around the world. Note that his form is right on the money with his weight balancing the boat fore and aft and sail shape excellent for high speed reaching.

~~5~~

. . . and Stones

In my experience, all small cats are very sensitive to weight and its placement. If the weight is in the wrong place, it can make a tremendous difference in your position in a race. You may be wondering why the other guys are screaming past you. What the other skippers are doing is reducing water turbulence at the rudder, or increasing the waterline, or making for better entry through the water, or getting more lift from their hull design, all depending on the point of sail they are on and the conditions that exist.

Let's head for the weather mark. If the air is light, the water will be fairly smooth with little or no wave action. In such a case the best possible place for your crew to be sitting is on the leeward hull and well forward. You should remain on the windward hull but inboard a little bit—and as forward as you can possibly get and still have good control over the steering of the boat. Since you have light air and flat seas, you have no worries over "hobbyhorsing" (up-and-down fore and aft movement encountered in waves). Your concern is to get a proper blend of lift from the flat hull midsections, minimum turbulence from rudder and exit hull portions, and maximum resistance to leeway.

By putting your crew weight a bit on the leeward side and forward, you are allowing the lee hull to bite deeper, and it will have something of the effect of a centerboard. It also helps keep shape in your jib. If you have been brought up on a monohull without full-battened sails, this is right up your alley. In addition—and most important—you are bringing your sterns up out of the water, eliminating turbulence and drag.

You could put your crew too far up on the bow and bury the hull, but, of course, you realize that you can overdo a good thing. When the crew complains that he has to change his diapers, ask him to move a smidgeon rearward until the bow is very low to the water but not under it.

In a Shark, Shearwater, P-Cat, or other boats that have splash rails in front, you have to be cautious about getting the rail itself in the water, as it is obvious that the rail would create more turbulence than you could ever save by lifting the rudder clear. You need a brake like this as much as a mailman needs a walk on his day off. A similar problem can develop with the fairly wide roll edge overhang seen on Hobie hulls.

On the Tornado and other cats with no splash rails, this little trick can be carried to utmost effectiveness. The Tornado has a particularly sharp and deep bow entry that can really act much like a centerboard when pressed deep in the water.

Now that you have all this down pat and can really move that boat in light air, along comes a chop. It could come from current, from witchcraft, or most likely from a stinkpot. Now this formula will not work too well unless you get your crew aft. He should now be sitting about in the same position as you are on the other hull. Still, both of you must be as far forward as you possibly can be, unless of course the bow is going under the chop. In that case, keep moving back until you find the point where the bow slices best through the waves with the least amount of hobbyhorsing. All cats have a rocker, a pivot point fore and aft. This can be seen clearly on cats without boards, and, on conventional cats, it is usually the center of the daggerboard. What you are after is to get your weight just enough ahead of the rocker to lift the transoms, but not so far that your weight becomes a lever, increasing the hobbyhorse effect.

In these conditions it would also be wise not to try to sail quite so close to weather, but rather to fall off a bit to keep your drive through the chop. That will also help in reducing the rocking effect on the boat.

The Tornado is much more easily handled in this ridiculous sort of sailing condition, as her sleek hulls really cut nicely through the waves, and the waves can usually find nothing to smack up against except the front beam, and that is pretty far aft. Sharks, Phoenixes, P-Cats, and the like, with those blasted spray rails, keep slapping the water in chop, and this—plus the tremendous forward buoyancy of the hull design (very useful in different circumstances) —causes much more hobbyhorsing.

In the case of these other cats with buoyant hulls and water guides of one nature or another, you will find it most important to concentrate the weight of both you and your crew exactly over one point on the boat, generally at the rocker. What you are doing is trying to utilize the same principle as that of one of those punching-bag clowns we used to have when we were kids. If you can remember, they were inflated and about the height of the kid himself. The clown was weighted perfectly and heavily in the middle. When a kid hit it, it fell partially over but would spring back past its original position (giving the poor kid a black eye on occasion) and then right back to rest where it was before it was clobbered. That is what you are trying to get your boat to do: resist the blows from the waves and spring back quickly when overcome. In this case you are trying to be the weight and not the clown. By keeping the weight of both you and your crew over the same point in the boat (fore and aft), you are reducing that pitching moment.

Now it's the second race and the wind has picked up to over ten knots and you are able to move well. The seas are still calm as in the previous example and your first leg is to weather.

At this point you must make a judgment whether or not to have your crew on the leeward side. You still want the leeward hull to be slightly lower than the windward hull, and you want the bow deep but not meeting with any resistance as it slices through the water. Since it is smooth water, you will probably have your weight very far forward. If the wind is strong enough to press the leeward hull lower, then it is probably an advantage to bring your crew back to the windward hull. (On some cats that do not carry a lot of buoyancy forward, crew can be most effective in the trampoline toward center and forward.) If he is on the windward hull, he might well lie down, stretched out forward on the hull, reducing his wind resistance while getting the bows deep in the water, thus allowing better windward work. The purpose of this maneuver is still to keep the stern up and away from drag and turbulence—all in a comfortable, low-profile position.

The minute the boat is sailing too flat, however, move your crew back toward the leeward hull.

The bows should be riding deep and giving lift to weather

with the sterns clear of the water. But now that the air is up a little, the boat may tend to bury the bows, so watch that the effective waterline is not too high on the bows.

By the time you have rounded the leeward pin, let's suppose that little wind you have been enjoying has kicked up a moderate chop. The position of your body will certainly not be in the same place as it was on the last weather leg, even though the wind conditions are the same. As in the case with powerboat chop, you should get your weight back and evenly over the hulls. If you are both on the windward side, one of you should sit in the inner deck (inboard of the hull on the trampoline) while the other sits on the hull as close behind as he can get. Remember, be the weight, not the clown.

Your next day of racing is different; this time the wind is blowing good and strong. It had just come up early in the morning, though, and the sea is still relatively smooth. It will be more than likely time to fly a hull, and a trapeze will be in order if you carry one on your boat. If the wind is not quite of a velocity to warrant a trapeze, you should have your crew sitting next to you and you should be sitting about in the area of the centerboard trunk (the rocker) or just slightly ahead of it. Your crew will be sitting just aft of the front beam. Even though there is no chop, sitting together will not hurt.

If the trapeze is used, the crew should be in the same position fore and aft on the boat—in effect, standing right behind you.

Now you really have to watch that the leeward bow does not tend to start down in these winds. If it does, immediately adjust your crew and your weight aft a hair. Keep moving back until you find a good balance point and the hull stops tending to dive. Your boat speed will now be up (along with your adrenalin) and you will just have to risk some turbulence at the rudder and move aft.

Now, on your second weather leg, there are some seas running. First, presuming your crew is not on a trapeze, you both should huddle up like Hansel and Gretel (even if you don't love him) in one lump and outboard as far as possible. That should aid in reducing pitching as well as heeling over too far.

If the trapeze is used, the monkey on the wire would be directly behind you. A good idea here is to have your crew spread his (or her) legs just far enough to allow you to lean back against him. In this way, you have put all your weight in one conglomerate and outboard as far as possible. You will not even have to use hiking straps in that case.

The next thing to watch is the leeward bow and how deep it is diving into the waves. In the case of boats with those clever appendages on the bow, you will see the splash rails really bashing into the waves and slapping about. Here you should get your weight quite a bit more aft but still together, reducing the problems that cause hobbyhorsing. With the clean entry, as in the Tornado, the demand to get aft is not so urgent, but keep a careful eye on the general reaction of the bows to the waves. When you find the front beam smashing into the waves, you must know it's time to move back some. Of course, you should never have let it go that far in the first place. In the heavier airs, you are generally looking for an even plane of the hulls through the water. If you are pitched forward, as you are in light air, the hulls will tend to dig and trip themselves.

~6~

With the Wind Behind

You have just rounded the weather pin and are starting off on that reach. If you remember your weather leg, you were sitting with the crew on the leeward side and forward to the bow for the light-air, smooth-sea position. By all means, do not change positions, for the same weight balance will be ideal for the off-wind work.

Even though the boat will have a little more drive on the reach, it will not be enough to drive the hulls so deep as to bury her bows in this light air. Another advantage to this position is that your crew is in the perfect spot to control sail shape in your jib by the most direct means known—by hand. His weight is well forward of the main beam and he is also in the right spot to see and trim the jib. If you can reach your tiller extension, you should be sitting on the windward hull in the same approximate area.

Here again you are diminishing the drag created by the rudder assembly and sterns. You may be creating a little tendency to "track" or lift to weather at a time when you would just as soon make a bit of leeway, but raising your boards in this case may neutralize that. However, if you find that in raising the boards you have developed a good deal of helm, then drop them back down either partially or all the way. You might try dropping the windward board first partially, then all the way if you still have some helm. You should definitely not need two boards unless you are on a very close reach.

Much as in going to weather, you still want your leeward hull a little lower than your windward hull. This will help sagging sails that can't get enough air to breathe to hold shape and reduce aft turbulence.

If a chop should develop, your concerns are less than on the weather leg as it will more than likely come from abeam or abaft and will not have the harmful effect you got when going to weather. You should still make sure your bows do not go too deep, at any rate. Should the chop in question be boat chop, it could come from anywhere—even a few feet in front of you. I recall a real drifter at Sandusky, Ohio, when a large fleet of Sharks, Thistles, and Interlakes were bobbing around, skippers holding their breaths so as not to disturb any of the wisps of air that might come their way, smoking cigarettes vehemently only to watch the blue, silky smoke rise straight up. When to their wondering eyes should appear a water skier streaking right through the whole bunch of us, seemingly using our masts for slalom marks. The happy skier was promptly upstaged by a fleet of those flag-carrying, card-bearing, thumb-sucking Power Squadron boats on maneuvers, blasting through the fleets in formation, waving buffoonish greetings at us while we went under for the third time.

So if it's boat chop coming at your bow, adjust as you would in going to weather: Move to a semiforward position, but most certainly both together or directly over the same position on opposite sides of the boat.

Togetherness is sometimes a necessity as shown by this skipper and crew huddled together on the aft crossmember, downwind at the Hobie 16 North Americans sailed in the near hurricane weather off Florida in 1974.

Now, under the supposition that the wind has picked up to a moderate blow but the water has remained fairly calm, you would do well to remain in the previous position—weight forward and slightly leeward. Since your crew is still holding your jib leads by hand and being a human barber hauler, he will naturally remain in that position under these circumstances. There should be no need as yet for him to move aft. If the wind force should begin forcing the bow under on occasion, then move him back as much as necessary—but no more.

With wind comes chop, and when it comes, move back—together. As skipper, you have the job of keeping a watchful eye on the stern and making certain it is out of the water. When the stern is down in the water, you are generally creating turbulence and drag behind the boat. You can almost watch it, observing the reduced stern wave when the water flow is allowed to come together before the blunt transom. Be sure, whenever possible, that you have the stern up out of harm's way. Of course, you can't do this at the expense of the bow's dipping or burying.

You might even keep your ears attuned for the sounds of turbulence—excess gurgling coming from the stern. If you move forward enough to press the bows, the gurgling should lessen or stop—unless, of course, you forgot to put in the plugs, in which case you can look forward to a great deal more gurgling.

Now the next race, and things have changed considerably as you are sailing along in heavy, hull-flying weather. Yet, by some miracle, the seas are still flat. This may happen all too seldom, but it does occur when good offshore breezes blow over sheltered bays. It is definitely worth consideration.

By now, your crew is on the windward hull alongside. Exactly where you sit is dependent on wind force and your true heading relative to the wind. What you should be looking for in ballast trim is a level planning effect as the boat slices through the water. In order to do this, you will probably have to move to the windward stern and hike out or trapeze. If a double trapeze is legal, use it. The forces of the wind are going to try to drive that leeward bow underwater. You must counteract that force by hiking or trapezing kitty-corner to that force on the leeward bow. The net result should be a flat-riding cat.

In contrast to your tactics in light air, you are trying to get the boat to ride flat. When I say "trying," I mean *trying*, for it cannot be done. But the trying will keep the boat in a slight heeling position with leeward bow deep and transoms nearly out of the water. Because the seas are flat, you can risk sailing fairly close to the point where your bows will bury. With that picture in mind, you should be reminded of the position you were trying to get when sailing in light air and flat seas.

There is a problem here, however, if the bow gets too deep. It will dig in and stop the boat in a frothy attempt to dive or submarine. That can be a very undesirable effect, even though it may not lead to an out-and-out pitchpole capsize. All the tripping will do is constantly slow you down while your competition sails on by. In boats such as the Hobie 16 and Unicorn, with minimum reserve buoyancy forward, this can be a real race-loser. You will simply have to abandon concern for rudder and transom turbulence and sit as far aft as possible. On the Hobie, your crew can trapeze completely aft of the rudder crossbar, even supporting himself on the hull rather than the trampoline.

To counteract the tripping and excessive hull flying, and to avoid the extreme cases of capsize and pitchpole, start easing the sheets, assuming that you are hiked out as far as possible. On reaches, I prefer easing the jib first along with a slight bit of mainsheet, adjusting them in order to reduce helm of any kind.

As for attempting to keep the transoms out of water in

heavy air, forget that one, for now you are trying to get the bows to drive through the waves and not take a dive. Some multihulls (particularly in the eighteen-foot-and-under category) will not hesitate to pitchpole forward when their bows get under at all. It is indeed a very uncomfortable and violent way to go.

Dr. Parrish Garver of Mentor, Ohio, was out sailing on Lake Erie one day in not too heavy air in a Cal Cat. The Cal Cat, a fourteen-foot, cat-rigged beach boat, was one of the early small designs by Carter Pyle and was quite a nice little boat. But, like many of the early small designs, she was a bit unstable in her fore-and-aft balance. Dr. Garver, an experienced catamaran sailor of everything from Sharks to Iroquois, managed to go popping right over the bow, breaking his nose, a rib, his glasses, and his pride. Beware the bow-burying boat!

Back to our sailing. Those smooth seas can't last long, and sure enough, the chop comes up, and again a minor change in your positioning. The worse the chop gets, the closer you and your crew should get to each other—and probably farther aft. With a choppy sea running, your bows will dive more easily, as the water is actually coming up to meet the bows.

Again, as in the flat sea with heavy air, after using all your ability to hold the boat flat with crew weight, you will most definitely have to start easing sheets in order to keep the boat on the right plane.

When you come to downwind sailing and you are no longer on the reach, then it's a whole new operation. Even though you are truly still reaching, it is a very deep reach and one with much more stability.

Here, in this chapter, we shall be discussing weight place-

Tacking downwind at its best—sails very full and drawing through an even slot; twist-off at the top of both main and jib similar; weight distribution is well forward but bows are well out of the water.

ment in downwind sailing. Sail shape and tactics are covered in Chapter 10.

You may wonder: Downwind? Why not sail wing and wing? Quite frankly, I cannot even discuss sailing downwind in this fashion in a catamaran. I have made a very deliberate attempt to know nothing about it. I made a decision a few years back that I would seldom, if ever, sail a catamaran dead downwind, wing and wing, or by the lee. It was my decision at that time to tack downwind no matter what the case. I can honestly say that, after a few years of practice and steadfastness, that decision has paid off. Certainly I have lost a few spots with my stubborn adherence to the idea, but I've gained far more than I've lost.

We are now sailing downwind as deep as we dare without giving up boat speed or sailing into a stall. The air is light and the seas are flat. Your crew must be as far forward as possible and you along with him. This is an ideal situation for your crew, for now he can reach and easily hold that sail shape in the jib. Your bows are deep and your transoms are up. This position is nearly the same as a reach.

As chop comes up, you will change your position only as little as necessary to keep the bows from diving. Again, you and your crew should sit exactly opposite one another on the hulls in order to reduce hobbyhorsing. You are still striving for the low and deep bow and the raised transom aft. In either case, flat sea or chop, it is preferable to have the centerboards up in order to give as much leeway as possible. While this may sound atrociously unorthodox, remember that the same attitude of the boat that allows leeway is allowing you, in effect, to point higher than the course you are sailing; that is, to reach more than to run and still make a running course. Your deep bow entry is fighting this leeway, so the elimination of a centerboard is most important if you are trying to make speed in this crabwise attitude.

Now take the downwind situation in moderate air and flat seas. Unlike your concerns on the reach, try to stay nearly in the same position as in light air. Depending on the wind force, you may have to move slightly aft to guard against bow burying; however, having both hulls in the water may help you. When a cat drives off deeper from its broad reach position, in the absence of sideways pressure, the windward hull stays down and helps with its buoyancy to hold the bows up.

If you can, try to stay forward. When the boat tries to dive, head her deeper—even if it's a momentary heading. This will give the boat a chance to stabilize and the windward bow a chance to bring its buoyancy into play, and instantly the bows will be back to the depth you want them. A warning here: Do not let the boat stall and slow too much when driving deep. You may have trouble getting her back up to optimum boat speed. Start back higher toward the reaching position the instant you feel the boat beginning to stall. Don't wait till she grinds to a halt.

If things are still not going right for you, even after heading deeper, have your crew move ever so slightly aft and keep trying to reach deeper to overcome bow diving. Keep moving aft until you find the most desirable spot.

Now the wind is really blowing, but we're still in flat seas. When it comes to downwind work and you're off that screaming reach, my preference in weight distribution does not change except minutely. The primary consideration is still to prevent the sterns from dragging.

Nearly always on my Shark or Tornado, I keep my crew on the leeward hull in all but survival conditions. Here he can hold shape in the jib while I steer from the windward hull in a spot directly opposite. With smaller cats of less displacement, you may not be so fortunate and may have to huddle as far back as the aft cross member. When extremely heavy air is combined with heavy seas, we may move back a teensy bit to prevent the bow from going under in the next wave. Again, though, when she starts under, just head her deeper and watch her scream for a while. And while she's screaming, the bows are coming back up and skimming smoothly through the water at the proper depth.

The advantages to this manner of sailing are numerous.

You are practically on a run and hull-flying possibilities are almost nil, even in heavy air. Another feature: If there is a sea, your hulls can catch the waves better for surfing if you sit forward. So you can surf deep, and when you outrun the wave or lose it, head higher and gain boat speed on the reaching position until you can catch another wave. This has enabled California skippers—notably Hobie 16 sailors—to steal many a regatta.

In case you haven't got the message by now, you want to put weight forward enough to keep the bows down to the water—but not under—and transoms up and out whenever it's possible to do so and maintain steerage.

~7~

Sports Car Steering

A racing catamaran has the fantastic ability of a sports car in its steering. The touch on the tiller is so delicate that the slightest steerage off course can produce dramatic effects. Sometimes these effects are not at all pleasant, and you find yourself mumbling, "Why is he outpointing me?" or "How can he tack downwind so fast?" or "How can he smoke along in this light air?" or "Why can't I keep the hull at that attitude?" These frustrations are the ones that most often send people to the club bar scratching their heads.

Many's the time in an exciting race that two catamaran skippers have been slugging it out to weather when suddenly one skipper allows a minor distraction to keep him from properly tending the helm, and down the tubes he goes. In the Schenley Cup Races of 1971, held at Put-in-Bay, Ohio, among the lovely islands of western Lake Erie, Bill Curtaindale of La Salle, Michigan, had me to weather, beating for the weather mark. I was not in a safe leeward position at the time, but on that particular long leg I managed to notice a couple of lifts that he had missed, owing to a minor problem aboard his boat. I sneaked up to the safe leeward on him. The lifts happened quickly; I was lucky and reacted promptly. So, while he was freeing some sheet or something, he was not steering with 100 percent efficiency. In a high-performance craft you cannot afford this. It cost Bill his position and he had then to follow in my bad air through the entire reaching leg. On my boat, with no problems aboard, I could use the quick steering to my advantage. The same quick steering worked in reverse to hurt my competitor when coupled with a few seconds of inattention. The reason for the quickness in steering is the speeds attained in those high-performance boats. It could be easily compared to a formula sports car with its very direct, responsive steering and little movement required to make it react. While the catamaran compares to the formula sports car, the average monohull would fit more closely the image of the family car: Its steering is excellent, but often not crisp, quick, and responsive. In the early days of the importation of small European sports cars, Ken Purdy suggested, in his book *Kings of the Road,* that you steered a sports car, but you aimed an American sedan. While a sports car required a mere flick of the wrist, the family car might take a good deal of arm movement and time to respond.

My namesake in sailing, Dave White of Leatherlips Yacht Club in Columbus, Ohio, was good enough to let me skipper his Interlake at a local regatta against a number of top-ranked national sailors in the class. After two races, and much to my surprise, I found myself tied for second place against those class hotshots. No doubt Dave's boat was in top tune, and Dave crewed, but I suspect the tiller had a lot to do with it. I had been sailing constantly in high-performance catamarans, and my tiller hand was quite adapted to quick, responsive steering. By jumping into a boat with less responsive steering, I was better able to find that thin line we all seek in

The Hobie 14, with its limited buoyancy in the hulls, has proved an excellent teacher of our maxim, "Get your weight in the right place—or lose!" Note the well-forward and low posture on these two sailors, leading the pack.

sailing to weather. I was unconsciously using the feel that I had developed in my sports-car boats.

There were two good friends that sailed cats with me. One of them moved to a high-performance catamaran from an Aquacat, while the other moved down (pardon the expression) from a thirty-foot keelboat. In both cases, these boats on which they had previously sailed were basically their trainers. The Aquacat sailor was an excellent racer and developed a good record of wins, and took top honors in his class, while the other poor fellow just simply could not get it together. He tried new sails, go-fasts, gadgets; he read all the top books; but nothing helped. I believe he just had not developed a feel for the helm.

High-performance craft of any kind must certainly be the trainers of the supersailors, as Buddy Melges of scow fame, and now Olympic gold medalist, has borne out. The scow has speeds much the same as the catamaran's, and it also requires the sensitive hand of a sports-car driver.

You see a lot of good, small one-design sailors move to the big boats and do very well, but you do not see many big-boat sailors go to one-design and do well. They simply do not feel the boat properly through its pulse, the tiller. As the one-design is to the auxiliary, so is the catamaran to the monohull. It is all relative.

After steering a fast-reacting boat, you should be able to slip into a slower reacting boat and do very well, as you will be attuned to the sports-car feel for your boat, and your steering will be that much sharper.

This sharp new development of which I talk will make a significant difference in skippers and their helmsmanship. Catamarans may very well be the breeding ground of top skippers in the future.

All this is by way of acknowledging that I cannot teach you the feel of sports-car steering, nor can I emphasize too strongly the importance of your developing such a feel. It is developed through sailing and more sailing, racing and more racing, but I doubt that it can be taught. If you have just moved into catamarans, you have probably noticed it already and found it as remarkable as some other aspects of the boat. When you are screaming across the water on a beam reach, you will note that a careless (or deliberate) small movement in the helm will bring the bows around sharply. It should be obvious that this sort of abrupt change in a race would be counterproductive.

If you sail a Hobie Cat 14 or any of the other small cats, you will note that giving a very hard pull on the helm, such as one is tempted to do when coming about, has the effect of putting on the brakes. Catamaran rudders can cause severe drag when they are held sharply over, and this is equally unwise in racing conditions. Such movements in a Hobie 14 are sharply punished, as you will probably go into irons long before you come about. They are more dangerous in a Tornado because this boat, with more drive and momentum, is deceptively forgiving and will probably come about anyway. But when you compare what you have lost in footage to your more smooth and steady competitor, you will discover that this "putting on the brakes" has penalized you about as severely. Throughout this book we keep reminding you to change trim when you have excessive lee or weather helm. The reason for this insistence is the same: helm pressure is drag!

So the best I can recommend is very watchful, alert experimenting when you are leisurely day-sailing. The aim is to develop consummate smoothness and a feel that matches your boat. Find the minimum amount of helm required to bring your boat about in various wind conditions and do not exceed it in practice or competition. Practice rounding out around a real or imaginary mark from close-hauled to a reach or run. Observe that if you are too harsh with your helm in this maneuver, the boat will slow down radically and sink deeper in the water as the lift from the speed is dispelled. When you do it right, the boat will often seem to pick up speed, and height out of the water as well. Practice and practice and keep feeling!

～8～
Bang!

Many races are won at one precise moment when that eight-gauge cannon fires and the red flag goes up and flutters at your stern. That is the time when all men are supposedly equal. That is when preplanning for this equality may make you the winner, or the lack of preplanning may make you the loser. Even though many times you have seen a great sailor come late for a start and still win the race, that is the exception and certainly not the rule. It is important to plan your start, and plan it well: Unless there is a major wind shift, execute your plan flawlessly.

Let's go back to the beginning of things, back to the simple handling of the boat. On the starting line you will be required to maneuver your boat with precision; to accelerate fast, stop fast, feather up, reach off, or whatever the game plan or circumstances the starting line may dictate. Make certain you can handle all these maneuvers and anticipate as many of them as possible.

Getting the boat to stop quickly while screaming along can be a bit difficult, but should be practiced until it becomes simple. Assume you are close reaching toward the starting line and want to stop. You must have enough room above you to head up and luff the boat. As soon as you decide to stop, let off both sheets and head up into the wind. You do not want to tack, so be certain that you do not head too high into the wind or you may end up having to flop. If that has not worked, in addition to heading up and easing sheets, push the boom to the leeward side beyond the point of the wind and backwind it. That will be your insurance against an accidental tack and at the same time add a tremendous brake. After practicing this maneuver, you should be able to stop on a dime. The same procedure, by the way, can be beneficial in landing at a close-quartered dock. For still more braking power, the jib can be backwinded by the crew, but to the weather side.

Most catamaran sailors will find it fairly easy simply to let the sails out and sit still without moving in any direction. With the combination of tiller, main, and jib you have plenty of steering devices to control the boat completely. Picture yourself sitting there, mainsheet out and the main with no draw, the same with the jib. You have the tiller pushed alee to keep the boat from wanting to reach off. You may notice that you have gone too high in trying to stop the boat and are nearing the point where you are into irons. Quickly pull on your tiller and sheet the jib. The combination of these two acts will bring the bows quickly away from the eye of the wind, and just as quickly go back to tiller alee and jib luffing before you gain any speed. The object is to keep the boat in a parked position.

I sometimes use an unusual starting technique that takes advantage of the catamaran's unique ability to back up. The object of this technique is to place my boat in the ideal spot on the lay line to the mark without critical timing and in a somewhat sneaky and unobtrusive manner. You may never want to try it yourself, but on the other hand, there are times when you may want to back up. Suppose you sail to a point 'way too high of the line and you have quite a bit of time and do not want to lose your place. Back up and you will be in a great position, with the competition right where you want them. By using the same technique as in stopping, push the boom alee once more, and watch the old boat go backward. Hang on *tightly* to the tiller, for the pressures exerted on the rudders may wrench it from your grasp, and breaking something in your steering mechanism is possible—a helluva way to start a race. In addition, if you wish, you may again have the crew backwind the jib, but it's not entirely necessary, unless you're in a hurry. It might be pointed out here that this technique makes a very good way to leave a crowded dock in tight quarters.

Catamarans certainly do sail well backward, by the way. Every year at Put-in-Bay, Ohio, at the ILYA Bay Week Regatta, the Interlake class holds a fun race called SWIM, CYCLE, SAIL, GUZZLE RACE. Skipper and crew must start at the gun, chug-a-lug one beer each, jump on tandem bicycles and pedal about a half mile to the lakeside, dive in and swim to their boats, hoist the sails, and race a windward-leeward course. This idea, dreamed up by the local PIBYC commodore, Bill Jellison, brought a huge influx of Interlakers. In 1969, when the Sharks held their nationals at nearby Sandusky, we Sharkers challenged these fun-loving sailors to a race in which we would sail backward on the leeward leg. But, much to our chagrin, they had enough fears of our hitting them going forward. They heartily declined the backward thing. Too bad; we could have done well. One Shark sailor claimed he could even sail up the weather leg backward.

Now that you have the hang of stopping, sitting, and backing, the next simple step is to get her truckin' again. Remembering that you should not be too close to the eye of the wind, you simply have to harden up your jib, follow closely by the hardening up of your main, and away you go!

Ideally, somewhere between stopping and truckin' is a good approach speed to the line, where you have good progress and lots of steerage, and—with a few grunts—you can be truckin'.

The best way to make sure you don't get into irons is to ride your jib up to the line. Then all it takes is the main to get you under a full head of steam. Approaching the line usually ends up an in-and-out affair with the sheets, in order to go faster, then slower, then faster, then slower, and on and on. The closer you are to good balance between the sails, the better, but you must be certain you do not go above close-hauled. That is the reason for the recommendation of relying primarily on the jib.

Now that you have all these practice maneuvers under your belt, picture yourself getting ready to head out for the big race and the start. *Do not forget your watch!* Don't forget your boat, either, but *do not forget your watch!* A watch is very important. There are some very good sailors who do not wear watches, and go by the drop of the pennant thirty seconds before the start, but it is difficult to commend such procedures. The ideal situation is to have your crew be the timer, calling off the minutes and seconds. Always be sure you are following your own watch as well, but try to make this a crew function. Good watches that are easy to see and read, preferably worn on the right wrist (on starboard tack this is the hand that holds the sheet), can make that nervous countdown before the start much easier on the ulcer. I may sound like some kind of "watch nut," especially when I admit I quite often wear three watches. I wear my regular watch to tell what time of day it is, but it has no sweep second hand, and I use a specialty yacht timer for the start, which reads only minutes and cannot tell the time of day, and I wear a stopwatch-type yachting timer around my neck, in case my wrist timer stops.

It is best to get out to the racecourse early and sail the weather leg, looking for any peculiar shifts near certain shores or islands, and any possible obstacles or holes that may be lurking between the starting line and the weather pin. This also gives you and your crew a chance to get some of your rust worn off. By sailing the leg up and back you may pretty well be able to determine which side of the course you prefer, if any. While sailing this leg, pick out landmarks on the lay lines and on various tacks, as well as using your compass to determine when you are on a lift and when you are on a header. In that way you will know, when the starting gun fires, whether or not you are sailing a lift or a header.

Now, back at the starting area, using your knowledge of the wind that you're on, sail off both pins, watching all the other boats doing the same, and that will easily show which pin is the favorite (closer to the wind). Keep in mind that the favorite end may well change at any time with a wind switch, so watch carefully for such a shift.

The best way to figure your tactic for any given start is to determine where you want to be after the gun goes off, whether starboard or port tack, and which side of the course you want to sail, or if you want to go up the middle.

In small fleets you can afford to be much more radical in your approach to the line. Suppose the starboard end is fa-

I'd rather have a late start than to begin in the middle of pack like this. You can wait for a start, but try to wait in clean air with your eye on a hole to break through.

vored, and you do not have a sixty-boat fleet to worry about forcing you over the line early. Although only one boat will get a good starboard-pin start, there will not be sixty trying, but only ten. In a large fleet, you would be better off to go on down the line a bit (even though it is not a better start) and look for clearer air and less congestion. While your foes are getting untangled, you may be picking up valuable yardage and truckin' on in clear air. If you wish to get out on port tack right away with the same starboard-favored pin, you may even wait until everybody is out of the way, then slip across the line and off onto port tack while the rest of the group sails off into the horizon, backwinding the hell out of each other—absolute death in a catamaran.

Suppose there is a nice line set (unusual, but perfectly possible). Then you have your choice of the entire line to start. That boat starting at the port-pin end is just as likely to be in the lead as the boat at the starboard or anywhere in between. In fact, the boat in between has a better chance, as he can fudge on the line more than those on the ends. So where you want to be after the start is again the major concern.

If you again want to be off on port tack, you want the starboard end start or a late start for safe tacking off to port. In other words, you want to be at the starboard end in order to get off onto port tack without interference, and a late start up at the end of the line will allow this. If you wish to sail the left side of the course, on the other hand, you are just as well off near the leeward pin, where there will probably be a bit less congestion and clearer air. That is an ideal spot if you are anticipating a header somewhere up the weather leg. Up the middle could be called a compromise, but it puts you in the enviable position of being able to tack toward the shift that either side may or may not be getting. But, in any and every starting situation, remember that with a multihull, clear air can be everything. With clear air, and even a tack unfavored originally, you can open up a hundred yards on your competition in minutes.

The next sort of start would be one of those lines that are rarely set by race committees, for some odd reason, and that is a port-end–favored line. Port-end–favored lines keep the boats from barging in on the committee boat and causing ticklish situations in protest hearings. Some sailors think the starboard end of the line is always the closest to the weather mark, and would start there if the first leg was a port reach. So obviously if the line is even, this sort of chap not only will be there on the starboard end of the line, but will be the barger. If the line is set port-favored, you have three options: First, if you wish to stay on starboard tack, you can reach down the starting line, heading up just before the pin, and go; second, a start on port, depending on whether or not you have a large or small fleet; third, if you wish to be safely out on a port tack, start on starboard in the middle of the line and flop at the first opportunity.

Now let's go back and figure approaches to these starts. With the situation of a starboard-favored line, you can figure by either compass or landmarks what is the lay line to make the committee boat while close-hauled. You want to be on that lay line within forty-five seconds of the start, or maybe a little higher. Do not get to the starting line too early, or you will surely get forced over and find yourself up the proverbial creek (without the paddle required by class rules). Work your way up slowly until you are within a fifteen-second dash of the starting line and cool it. Prepare to get under way quickly, for you will soon be attacked from above and below. With about ten seconds to go, bring in your sails and get her moving; hang back a few feet, and when there are five seconds left, strap her in and go. It should take that long for the boat to gain enough speed to cross the line, and by that time you will be right on it.

If you are indeed closest to the pin, you may want to pinch up a bit, forcing all those behind you to sail in your lee. Now, if all is right, you have a marvelous opportunity to tack off to port.

Keep in mind that starting next to the starboard pin (starboard-favored) is risky business. Everyone wants that spot. For insurance, you'll do better to stay away from that jam-up and get on down the line a few boat lengths, sacrificing some position for clearer air.

If you must get off on a port tack right away, you can camp right above the lay line and, after everyone else has cleared, fall off into the starting area, slip across the line, and quickly tack to port. This may seem like quite a sacrifice, but in reality it is not. While everyone is jamming up at that end of the line, you are simply waiting for them to get out of the way. After they remove themselves and backwind each other off on starboard, screaming obscenities at one another, you can slip in there, seconds behind them, and go off on your own breeze.

When the line is starboard-favored, there can be no good reason for going near the port-end pin. But in these circumstances the RC boat (obviously masochistic) should be as ironclad as the *Merrimac*, as it is quite likely to get rammed—and that should be considered the RC's own fault.

With the well-set line, it is merely a case of choosing where you want to be after the start and getting to that position along the line. You can use a little less cautious approach to the line, however, as you will not be worrying about bargers and leeward boats so much if you are not near the RC boat. Try to keep a nice hole below to fall into five to ten seconds before the start. Keep heading the windward boat up and threatening to push him across the line, and with ten seconds left, fall off, and with five, fire up your afterburner and get going. By the time you actually hit the line you will be moving well and into the hole you had saved for yourself. Remember, it's important not to wait until zero hour to harden up, for it will take you nearly three seconds just to start pulling the sheets. Even with the tremendous acceleration of a catamaran, five seconds is a conservative figure, unless you are almost over the line in the first place.

With the port-favored line, a good prerace procedure is to

sail the length of the starting line, carefully noting how long it took you to do so. Now, if you are going to make a starboard start on this port-favored line, you know where you should be and when. The pin you want to be closest to is the port pin, but don't be overly concerned about being right at it when the gun goes off, unless you are trying to knock a port-tacking friend. Getting within six or seven boat lengths of the mark will put you well out ahead of most of the boats, if not all of them.

Making your approach on this line, you should start just below the committee boat and act as if you are merely early for an even line, and you want to be near the starboard pin. This is particularly nice when a shift comes, making the line even starboard-favored. If that happens, you need only to park, or maybe sail backward a bit, and you are right where you want to be. When you have your running time down the line, plus about thirty seconds, fall off and get on down where you want to be. Do not get right on the line, but back behind two or three boat lengths. You may find an occasional boat that will try to force you over, but you have plenty of time and space and that shouldn't bother you, as you sail over him. If you were right on the line, that could mean trouble, particularly if the one-minute rule is in effect. (If the one-minute rule is in effect, no boat may be to windward of the starting line or any extension thereof after one minute before the start.) Keep on moving down the line with good speed, and with five seconds to go head up and go for the line. The bigger the fleet, the sooner you should leave your "parking area" at the starboard end and head for the port end, for in the big fleet you may get forced over early about three-quarters of the way down.

Another approach—and a dangerous one—is the port-tack

start. There are certainly occasions when port tack is the only way to go. If you are in need of a good race, and can pull it off, that's the way to go. However, if you're in the lead and have only to cover someone, you shouldn't chance something so radical. In small fleets, port tack is no sweat, for it's easy to fall into a hole and/or duck under a few boats, if you should not be able to make a successful port-tack start right at the pin.

The timed start is the best way to get off on a good port-tack start, if you want it at the port buoy. Sail away from the port starting mark on starboard tack and on a beam reach. Try to leave the mark with one minute and fifteen seconds to go. Sail out on starboard for thirty more seconds, jibe, taking approximately fifteen seconds, and make it back to the starting-line pin within the remaining thirty seconds. You will be hitting the line on a full-speed beam reach and need only to harden up, head up, and go. The oncoming starboard boats will probably have been luffing down the line and will take a few seconds to get a full head of steam, while you are boiling away. Be sure to head up fast when you pass the pin. You'll be surprised at how far that reaching speed will carry you uphill after rounding up.

You can probably do the port-tack shot from a luff, but you are better off to have a good run at it, for you need all the advantage you can get in the speed department.

If things get really tight and you have no way of making it at the pin, bear off and reach off down the line until you spot a hole and can duck into it. Ducking under sterns will not be as bad as you think if you are getting to the right side of the course. Another way to kill time is to make a 360-degree tack before reaching the pin, and try again after your jibe. Most of the boats will be trying to go to port at their earliest convenience and room may be made quickly.

There are as many successful starting techniques as there are starters. If these techniques, especially adaptable to multihulls, don't work for you, don't hesitate to pick up on your reading from any number of good monohull sailing writers and build your own adaptation.

~9~
Going Up!

Personally I am no big believer in developing and setting up such a thing as a "weather boat." I certainly do believe that developing the ability to sail the weather leg *well* is a must for the ardent racing sailor. The ideal is to have a fairly versatile boat with tendencies to be superior for off-the-wind sailing, and then develop one's abilities to sail the boat to weather. In that way, you put yourself among the leaders of the race and up in the clear air on the weather leg, rather than being buried in the avalanche of agitated air in the middle of the fleet. Then when you round the weather mark and start your reach, you need only to set up for your off-the-wind work and pass up all those "weather-tuned" boats. When sailing on the next leg, you have only to cover.

Assuming you are already off the starting line and fairly well into clear air (getting into that clear air is a *must*), be sure to keep that clear air by looking constantly for holes in the fleet to get through or to get more to the favored side of the course. Try to stay in clear air all the way up the weather leg. If you are being backwinded by a safe leeward boat or catching gas from a leading windward boat, you will cer-

It's a good time for Shearwater no. 204 to tack or drive off as you may be sure that the lead boat will continue to widen its lead in a parade like this.

tainly be in a bad way at the weather pin.

So, in working your way through the fleet, try your damnedest to keep clear air. You will do infinitely better than the hotshot in the "go to weather" machine, who will be busy in the center of the fleet demonstrating how high and fast he can point.

Most racing catamarans. that utilize a jib should sail to weather by it—and it alone. It's your guide. The jib and the main must complement one another, but, for the sake of helmsmanship, the jib is the sail of the hour on the weather leg. Depending on the wind and waves, it should be set either hard, slack, or somewhere in between. But the principle in any case remains: You *must* sail the boat by the jib.

Your crew should have the jib set for the wind and the wave condition as required and then cleated. Yes, I said cleated! Cleating is mandatory if you are to use the jib as a bellwether of boat efficiency. Many excellent sailors might argue that point, but in the case of a catamaran, there should be very little dissension. Remember, it's very hard to read a full-battened main with its fixed port or starboard camber. It takes quite a luff before you will discover you are out of trim, no matter how many streamers you fly. Suppose your crew is holding the jib as you are beating and is constantly adjusting the sheet, as he well might be in a slow-moving monohull. That sounds really impressive—makes you think grandiose things about hard-working crewmen who never falter. In most cases, however, this constant adjusting is messing up your ability to sail to weather.

As I've mentioned, the boat sails by her jib. Therefore, it is improbable that the skipper can successfully drive the boat consistently with an ever-changing jib setting. It's not a partnership. It will be very difficult. The crewman, responding to every wind shift with a jib adjustment, blinds the helmsman from the useful information that the jib can provide.

Suppose the wind should head you five degrees while you're sailing close-hauled. The jib begins to luff. If the jib is cleated, the skipper would fall off five degrees, keep sails drawing and the boat driving. That is what should and would occur with a cleated jib. If instead your hard-working crewman should pull the sheet in tightly, he would be changing the jib's position relative to the main, resulting in a jib much too flat for the situation and backwinding the main. The skipper would pinch to weather instead of driving the boat. Even if the helmsman were to drive off a bit—knowing more than his crew—with the distorted position of the jib, it will not be enough to compensate for the directional change of the wind. The boat will be in the attitude of pinching.

In another case, let us suppose that our hard-working crew is still at it and you get a little lift. The crewman does not want you to be overtrimmed, and so eases the sheet. This case may not be so disastrous for the sail complement as the case of a header, for now the jib will do no actual violence to the main. But the boat is not sailing to optimum performance and that is nearly as detrimental. A shift has been missed that you could have well used, and you sail on your way never knowing what you lost.

In the competitive world of Tornado and Hobie racing, this can kill your chances of coming near a trophy. That may allow the boat below you to move up into the safe leeward, and the next time there's a header you're dead; you will suddenly be sailing in garbage air.

There will be times when you get back to shore and hear such things as "Boy, does So-and-so ever point high and still foot!" Balderdash! The competitor was merely sailing the boat to weather properly.

What are the ingredients for sailing the boat to weather properly? Helmsmanship is important. You want to steer the boat on its most efficient weather course—not too high, not too low, right on target—the very thin line of perfection. Normally, when a boat is pointing too high, it will gain very little speed forward; if it is not pointing high enough, it may go fast but not in the right direction. But when it is sailed properly—sails set to complement one another, jib cleated, walking that very thin line of steering—it will be one of the first to that weather pin.

I advocate the cleated jib for another simple yet all-important reason. The modern catamaran has a very small jib in relation to the main. It is important in a Tornado, a Shark, or a Hobie to make the main work—not to make it subservient to the very much smaller jib. With the jib cleated, it is now the entire duty of the skipper to keep sails full and drawing out of any luff or stall. And his crew is helping him by giving him the best information on which to act. An over-zealous crew can trim the jib perfectly yet help the skipper to throw away the very much larger mainsail.

Driving far off can sometimes be a good idea, but not as a general practice. Footing is all-important in multihull racing, and yet most sailors do not foot their boats, but usually pinch. In some circumstances it might be advisable to drive the boat off below a degree of heading that would be considered "good footing off." This could be useful in choppy seas in light air (when such a technique would keep the sails from flopping around) or in choppy seas in heavy air, which pitch the boat extremely.

This might be an opportune time to mention the technique of sailing in heavy winds and seas. First, flat sails are in order. Although you may opt for a full sail in every other instance, that fullness can now hurt you, as we discussed in the chapter on the mainsail. Get out those stiff battens and get things flattened out as much as possible. Stiff battens at the top of the sail are particularly good.

Next is technique. Most of us have learned somehow along the way that the traveler should be eased off center so that you can drive off and through the waves better, without fear of hull flying and its consequent wasted effort. Part of that is correct. Yes, you should drive off more, possibly even past the point of good footing in the heavy going, for that allows you to blast through the waves. And yes, the sails should be somewhat eased, as this will allow you to run off "free" in the sea. But instead of easing the traveler, here you should be easing the mainsheet. With the stiff battens, the top of the sail will respond to the eased mainsheet and twist off much easier than with softer battens, which tend to put fullness at the top. With this twist-off, you will have reduced your heeling moment while allowing the bottom of your sail to keep up its tremendous power (very much needed to drive you through the waves).

If you have too little power in your main, you will find yourself hobbyhorsing (wasted motion), while if you have too much, you will constantly be having to feather the boat up. A great deal of experience for the feel of the power of the mainsail is necessary to know how hard to sheet.

In the monohull, for example, sheets are eased, but to lower the heeling moment, the traveler is one of the first to be eased. Then you feather up into the wind. In a catamaran, the traveler is never eased going to weather and you should fall off in order to drive through the waves; otherwise, you will go only slightly faster than a monohull, and that won't win a regatta. To reduce the heeling in a cat, the top of the main must twist off.

British catamaran sailors have often criticized their American counterparts for what they identify as an inability to see the seas for the waves. They infer that we treat each individual wave as a separate problem and not as one of a series that we must know is about to hit us the minute we have passed the wave of the moment. They suggest that good catamaran helmsmen should concentrate on the whole of the seas ahead of them. Set and hold as straight and steady a course as possible over a whole series of waves and chop. Unless the waves are favorable long rolling swells such as you might encounter in Southern California, Hawaii, and other parts of the Pacific, pumping the tiller to get over each individual wave will net you no profit—especially upwind.

With the exception of severe conditions, you will, however, avoid footing off excessively far—but avoid equally the opposite vice. If the skipper steers too close to the wind (a very common problem), the boat will be pinching again. From all appearances, the craft is really going to weather; in fact, quite the contrary is the case. Speed to the mark will be significantly slower than a "well-footed" cat. The slower speed allows more leeward drift as it moves through the water. Leeward drift will nearly always offset the difference in heading and the boat will end up at the same spot it would have if it had been sailed properly—only much later. Therefore, many boats that were behind you are now suddenly ahead.

Saying a boat is footing nicely is saying that it is not pinching or stalling off; it is walking that nice thin line you can get only from sailing by your jib in a cleated position.

Most catamaran skippers do pinch too much, and I can do you no greater favor than to continue encouraging you to steer off a bit more. You can even risk an exaggeration of that point of steering just to get a feel for the speed of a well-footed boat and to know how a catamaran is supposed to sail.

There are a few cases, however, where pinching slightly can pay off. In the unusual circumstances of very light air and very flat seas, and given a boat such as the Tornado, Hobie 16, or Sol Cat, where you can optimize lateral resistance by a shift of weight forward, one can pinch success-fully. But normally it's not a good idea.

In 1971 at the Great Lakes Multihull Championships, my crew, Larry Herold, and I were fighting it out with the entire fleet in a near no-air situation and glassy seas. We were well forward on our Tornado, putting the bows very deep, giving us a great deal of bite. We pinched unbelievably and ghosted away to a good lead.

Now we should deal with the hard-working, sheet-pulling crewman who used to mess up forward progress on the beat. Actually, the crewman has much to do. Of paramount importance, he must be certain to keep the weight distribution in the boat at the proper position. Since the skipper is married to the tiller and cannot move about as freely, the crewman must be used as movable ballast. The skipper and crew should, of course, be very close, to reduce any hobbyhorsing that might occur.

As skipper, your biggest contribution should be to keep your mind clear in order to sail the craft to its best abilities. You must be free to concentrate on the jib, the wind, the waves. Your crew should help you to relegate to the back of your mind such considerations as where the marks are, where the fleet is, and all about that one competitor that you must beat. To the extent that he can handle those problems, you can keep the boat moving.

If you have a really stellar crew, one you can virtually treat as a coskipper, you can leave tactical decisions almost totally up to him. With the average crew, you may have to be content with training him to feed you the information on which you can make sound tactical choices.

You should rely on your crew for intelligent information as to where the fleet is (hopefully behind you), what tack the other boats are on, where your main competitors are, where the weather mark is, any visible wind conditions, if you can lay the mark, when it might be advisable to tack for the mark—and, if he's really astute, where some of the boats may be getting a lift or a header. When I say "intelligent" information, I mean just that. Often you end up with a mouthy crew that could drive you up a tree even if you weren't trying to sail a race. If his reporting on other boats goes something like "Man, is Charlie ever outpointing us," or "Wonder why Willy is going so fast and we're going so slow," or just plain "Jeeeeeeeeezus," he may well put you in traumatic shock before you reach the weather pin. Next time leave that one ashore.

Talking about the party at the yacht club tonight does not exactly lead to winning races, either. Sailing a boat to weather requires a great deal of concentration. Study the winners in any big class: 470, Hobie, Star, what have you. What marks them is their ability to concentrate. A mouthy crewman can demolish concentration before a race is even started. Conversely, the right crewman can expand your own powers. Work with him or her. It may take a few races before you get him feeding you the proper balance of information and emotion, but work on it. It will be worthwhile.

Tactics with catamarans do differ in some cases from monohull tactics. The reasons for this are obvious: the high speed of the boats and the lack of ability to carry through a tack quickly. For example, two monohulls are approaching one another, one on port (slightly ahead) and the other on starboard. Tactically, the port-tack boat should not take a chance on making it ahead of the starboard boat and should tack right under the starboard boat, thus ending up in a safe leeward position. He will find himself still ahead and throwing bad air back up to the starboard competitor.

If two multihulls were in a similar situation, and the port boat tacked, the starboard boat would (because of its continued high speed of travel as opposed to the slow tacking speed of the port-tack boat) drive well over the port-tack boat and cover him completely.

Suppose the port-tack boat could even make it across in front of the starboard boat. The monohullist would very probably tack on top of the starboard boat to cover and blanket. Not so in the multihull, for by the time the port-tacker was by and tacked, the high speed of the starboard-tack boat under way and the slow tacking of the port-tacker would have combined to allow the starboard-tack boat to drive well through the shadow of the tacking boat, into clear air and a safe leeward position.

How do you keep that slight edge lead and avoid the above problems? There are two solutions open to the port-tack boat. The first requires a bit of preplanning. When the crew alerts you to a possible starboard-tacker, you should tack immediately and never get near him. Second, ease off and duck behind the starboard-tacker. You may grieve that now you are behind him, but your time will come on the next tack. If you both tack equally fast, you will now be on starboard and he will have to do the ducking behind and you will still be in the lead.

In another situation, your competitor is coming up to you on a port tack and you are on starboard. If you have a lead of at least three to four boat lengths, you might be able to flop and blanket him. If you don't have a sufficient lead, he will blow out the leeward side of you into a safe leeward—not good. Beware of making that mistake. You would do better to tack to a safe leeward of him than risk his doing it to you.

If, however, you have plenty of room and you can safely flop and get under way again in time to keep him from breaking through your lee, you may do so, but with another precaution. Do not sail very far above him to windward before flopping, or he will still be past your garbage air, and, though not in the safe leeward position, he will be on equal terms with you as far as the clear air goes. You may find you have tacked for no advantage.

A good guideline is to take an extension of his windward bow and tack one foot above that point where you sail across the extension of this line. The radius of your turn will put you even higher, but it also ensures that if you have to backwind, you will not back into his path and foul him. Now, when you tack, your wind shadow (which, by the way, streaks back as far as your apparent wind streaks forward) will strike directly on your competitor and you will move on in clear air while he wallows.

If you were on a starboard tack, nearing the pin but not laying it and needing to tack twice more, and a port-tacker is coming along, you might be tempted to do as the monohullist does and get over him—flop and cover the lay line. With a cat, that is not a great idea. If suddenly you find that you are only a boat or two ahead of him, your flopping will allow him to dive under you and into clean air—a safe leeward. Then he can, by driving off a bit, flop to starboard, and you are the one with no rights. In that particular case, I prefer to tack to port before I get to him, putting my boat ahead and to leeward. Then, when I reach the lay line to the mark, I flop to starboard and exercise my rights and sail on to the pin. The other fellow is left to duck behind me to tack or flop to starboard under me and let me drive over him. In either instance, we will leave him slopping around in our wake.

Excess tacking, in any case, should be avoided. For, as you have no doubt discovered with your first Hobie 14, most multihulls are very lightweight and overcanvased, and generate extremely high windage (counting both hulls); and with all that going for them, they come about relatively reluctantly.

Still, they are the fastest things on water (which is why we sail them), and with this factor in mind, one must carefully calculate when to tack and when not to. Monohulls should be tacked on nearly every header, as they can drive through the tack, virtually never missing a beat. The cat, on the other hand, has a great deal working against it in a quick turn of this nature, and, as forward motion nearly stops in the eye of the wind, tacking must be more carefully considered.

There is no doubt that you should consider tacking to headers, as any fine sailor might. But tacking loses time, and unless the shift is a fairly good-sized one, or if it aids you tactically, you would probably be wise to stay on your tack. Not that you should doggedly stay on one tack to the lay line and then tack to the mark. That could be disastrous. But keep your tacking to a sensible minimum. The fact that you are sailing to your jib will be a great help to your resolve to hold your tacks. This kind of sailing in a relatively fast multihull will mean that you will quickly make the most of any lift and minimize the effect of most knocks because you are at all times reading them for what they are.

We have talked about the slowness with which the catamaran tacks and its influence on your upwind strategy and tactics, but what of its speed? You can learn to use this speed, and you can do it best by not worrying about how high you—or the guy behind you—point. Sail your own race. As I suggested earlier in this chapter, let the boat foot off and drive. That pincher may look as if he's going to the pin, but when you tack (provided you do not tack to a lift, of course) you should find yourself well ahead of the pincher. That is using the speed of a cat. A pinching boat will have all he can do to equal monohull speeds. You will get there first.

~~10~~

Over the Hill

Sometimes it seems as if you will never get there, but as sure as the Lord makes little green apples, lifters, and headers, here you are approaching the weather mark on schedule.

Sometimes the next leg may be a very close reach. It damned well should not be, but if it is, you will have little to do in preparation for the next leg of the course except getting a bit farther aft on the boat. Some sailors, the minute they round any weather mark, like to inhaul their mains, allow their jib leads to go forward, or, if they have them, use barber haulers—all those little items that will make the sails fuller. However, that is really not a great idea on this point of sail, for you are really going to be just off a beat angle, and your sails should remain fairly flat. Whatever you have used in the way of fullness or flatness on the weather leg, as dictated by the particular wind, wave, and weight conditions, will continue to give you the best performance on a very close reach, with the sheets slightly eased. Fullness in your sails on a close reach will make for more hull flying, which entertains the spectators but is not very fast.

Your purposes would be better served by easing your main and jib sheets a smidgeon than by doing all the sail-setting alterations. By easing the sheets you are making the sails slightly fuller anyway, and you can hastily harden up when necessary—a puff, flatter seas, or, more important, a competitor trying to drive over you.

Again I want to point out that it is unusual that your second leg on any decent course would be a close reach. Normally, a close reach is encountered on the course after a major wind shift has come skulking over the course like Carl Sandburg's fog, on little cat feet. Close-reaching courses turn a catamaran race into a parade. Both race committees and competitors should avoid the temptation to look photogenic on such legs and shun them like the *unchallenging* plague they are.

More normally, if you are sailing on a real course in a real race, and are approaching the weather buoy, you know that you will have to round the mark and fall off to a beam reach or a broad reach, depending on whether or not the course is an equilateral triangle or a ninety-degree isosceles triangle. Setting up for the next leg can be done while you're approaching the mark, but you will usually find that you and your crew are too busy or too worried to start making adjustments yet. Perhaps the crewman could raise your weatherboard if you are somewhat above the mark and are sure to make it.

As you approach the mark, keep the jib drawing well, but start easing the main first—and fast! The mainsail has a tremendous steering power that can keep forcing the bows to weather, yet meanwhile you are trying to pull the bows leeward with the efforts of the rudders. Do not get the two of them working against each other. As you are rounding the mark, let the main completely out—particularly if the next leg is a broad reach—and pull the tiller bar. In this manner you are using your jib to help force the bow downhill; the main is not opposing the forces of the rudders, which are likewise forcing her downhill.

Danger! If you are going off onto a beam reach, you may want to stay a bit high after rounding so that no one drives over the top of you and makes you eat garbage air all the way across the reaching leg. However, if you know the next pin is pretty far below you, do not stay high too long. Remember the old maxim that what goes up must come down.

On beam reaches most sailors want to stay very high all the way across the leg, and they usually end up driving over a few boats, but when the time of reckoning comes (the reaching pin), they suffer badly coming back downhill, while the boats that had been driven over are rushing toward the mark with the inside overlap and with better speed. Even though it takes quite a constitution, reaching right at the mark or even a little lower can usually be pretty rewarding. There are occasions when the lucky devil that went high will get a fortunate puff and drive down quickly, much to your chagrin, but that is rare, and he still will not necessarily be ahead of you.

At the opening of this chapter we were discussing sail trim (or lack of it) on those occasions when the reaching leg is little more than a senseless continuation of the beat. Now, in contrast, sail trim on real beam reaches requires quite a bit of fullness. Your outhaul on the main could be released and your jib leads could be forward, barber-hauled if you have the equipment. On this point of sail you should not need a leech control wire, for it would create too much of a hook in the sail, and thus a windbrake. In lighter air your crew could be holding the jib lead outboard, but not too far forward, being careful to pull down on the leech of the jib to attain fullness. He should watch that he does not backwind the main under any circumstances. If the air is moderate to heavy, you do not want the crew weight to the leeward side of the boat, and so the use of the barber hauler or forward jib lead is called for.

If a puff hits and it becomes flying time on this point of sail, most ex-monohull racers have a bit of difficulty controlling the instinct to feather up to control the heeling of the boat. As in iceboating, the thing to do when the hull begins to fly is to fall off sharply and even sheet in, assuming you have done everything you can to hold the weather hull down with crew weight. The apparent wind now moves far forward, the hull begins lowering, and you will really smoke through the water.

It would be nice to reduce the wetted area of the boat, so lifting up a dagger board could be a good idea. The preference is toward raising the leeward board. The leeward board is where the maximum wetted surface is concentrated and where its reduction will be most effective. And this is where the board is acting as a fulcrum to hike the boat. Lift the board and sail flatter. You will still have your windward board to help your steering, but will be without the board that would make the hull fly so quickly. If steering becomes difficult, drop the idea of raising a board, for you are going to cause more drag by oversteerage and rudder resistance than you would otherwise reduce by raising the board.

We are going to talk about deep reaching now, so let's go back again to the weather mark. Rather than go off on that previous beam reach, head into a deep reach. In this case, as you round the mark the jib should be drawing as before, but as soon as you are past the point of a beam reach, let the jib sheet out all the way and have the crewman quickly get to the leeward side of the boat and hand-hold the jib. The mainsail, as before, should be most of the way out or all the way out. Working together, skipper and crewman should be able to get the sails very full and hulls very clean in just a few moments, without letting the sails flutter and without losing steering.

You are seeking to get the sails very full and the water drag reduced. You and your crew should have assignments when rounding the weather mark. The centerboards should be raised, the outhaul released, inhauler in effect, leech line applied, and downhauling devices eased. All this can be done in one clean sweep by skipper and crew after some practice. Each crewman should know his duties along this line. It's important to get these things accomplished, but not at the cost of steering the boat off into a stall or jibe, or letting the jib wave on the wire like a yacht club burgee. Look for a good full main and a good full jib, both complementing one another, and the least amount of underwater drag.

When you're rounding the weather mark and bringing both your boards up, if you should notice any difficulty in the steering, put a board down, preferably the windward board. Even though there should be less drag with both boards up, because there is less wetted surface, you may find your steering difficult. In this case, you are no doubt creating more drag with the boards up because you are having to pull on the tiller too hard for correct steering, thereby causing a water brake with your rudders, resulting in increased drag.

Your mainsheet traveler and main should be as far outboard as possible, and the sail as full as you can get it. A leech line will help in getting it fuller and may have the tendency to draw the draft aft in the sail, which is desirable. If you have a boom vang, you will find that it greatly increases the effectiveness of the leech line. But you can do without one by sheeting the main some to hold the boom down and letting the leech wire push the battens forward, making them bow and thereby increasing the fullness of the sail.

Many full mains, when set far outboard, will set up against the side stays and ruin the shape of the sail, and so you must trim the main sheet some until the crease made by the stay disappears and you have a nice full shape. Be careful not to overtrim the mainsheet, for you may begin flattening the big sail, which is not at all desirable on this point of sail. Once you have the main set the way you want it, that will be the last of the tending you have to do, and you may as well cleat it, for it will have no feel for the variables on the balance of the leg. It is easily uncleated if you must steer to a higher heading for some reason.

The jib should be hand-held, forward, outboard, and pulling down on the leech of the sail. The crewman should be aware of the shape of the main and make what attempts he can at holding the jib so that the leech of the jib takes on a curvature matching that of the main.

If the mark for which you are heading is straight ahead or a bit higher than the course you are steering, then the crewman should be adjusting the sail as you go along, making certain that it is not luffing or stalling. All the helmsman should have to do then is steer the boat toward the mark, and possibly trim his mainsheet when necessary. However, if the mark is below the course of steering, the crewman must hold the jib in one place while the helmsman steers by the jib, much as he does in going to weather.

The jib in this case, since the helmsman must rely on it to steer the boat, must be set just as carefully and properly downhill as it is when going to weather. The sail can be set too far forward, or too far aft. With the sail set fairly well in relation to the mainsail, you may rely upon telltales at the onset, but try to feel the boat speed after gaining some experience. Just like walking a boat to weather, you must also walk the boat downhill. There is a very thin line to walk: head too high and you will get boat speed, but you'll be heading in the wrong direction; head too low and you'll stall and die in the water.

As for telltales, you can use them on the diamond spreader, the side stay, and the luff of the jib (and on the mainsail aft of the luff and on trailing edges). The telltales on the side stays and diamonds are best used when the mark is directly ahead or a bit above, while the jib telltales should be utilized when the mark is below you. The diamond stay's telltales, as well as the side stay's telltales, should be pointing to aft of the mast a bit and more or less toward the leech of the main. But when the mark is below you, you should use the jib telltales and forget the others. Now you should sail your boat just as you did when going to weather.

If the weather-side telltales act up, then you should fall off, for you are going too high and thereby luffing. When the leeward side telltales begin to frolic, you are stalling the boat and should head back up higher (and while you're heading back higher, you'll notice that the boat speed will begin to increase). For catamarans, stalling the boat is far worse than luffing, with its effects on boat speed, although neither is desirable.

Try to get the feel of relative boat speeds. Just as in going to weather, you want to sail as close toward the mark as possible, but not lose boat speed in the process. There is a very thin line downhill; you must try to maintain your very best speed, but working the boat deeper and deeper all the time.

You may find yourself heading up for speed and then quickly falling off to get deeper, then back up for boat speed, then deeper again. Practice, and this steering will come to you naturally. This point of sail takes a great deal of concentration on the part of both the skipper and the crew: the skipper because he must feel his boat, keep it moving well, yet going as it can go without stalling; the crew, for he must tend his jib flawlessly, making sure that the leech of his sail is tight, that the sail is full and with good shape, and that it conforms to the main.

There is only one way to sail a leeward leg or deep reach, but somewhere someone has said that there is another way to go downhill: running wing and wing. To run wing and wing, put one sail out on one side and the other sail out on the other side, head for the mark with your barn-door effect, and get beaten. That is about all that can be said about it, except for one possible exception: In a gale it may be faster than tacking downwind.

The way to get to that leeward pin the fastest has to be tacking downwind. "Tacking" is something of a misnomer for the technique of jibing the boat downhill (zigzag course) in relation to the marks, much as you do in tacking to weather. In most cats you will find that to lay a mark dead downwind, you will need to sail at about 45-degree angles from the rhumb line to the buoy, much as in going to weather. There is a lay line, just as on the weather leg, which must not be exceeded. That is, you do not want to overstand any more downwind than you would want to overstand going to weather.

But let's go back to the weather leg now. Picture yourself approaching the weather mark with your next leg being a leeward course. As you round, steer deep immediately, getting your sails full and hulls clean.

Remembering to keep the boat speed and still heading as deep as possible all at the same time, try to think about whether you are now sailing on a header or a lift. Here, on this point of sailing, is where the best of us can get lost. On the weather leg, when you get headed, you want to tack to that header, for that will get you closer to the mark, and get you there faster. If you get lifted, you hang on to that tack, for it's getting you to the mark faster. Sailing downhill is the exact opposite of sailing to weather. When you are headed, it is really a lifter, that is, it is getting you closer to the mark. You want to take full advantage of that header and so you should hang on to that tack. When you are lifted on the downwind leg, you are being taken farther away from the mark, and so you should jibe to the lift, exactly opposite of the weather leg. One further difference worthy of note is that as you now tack, you are jibing each time, and—if your crew work is good—this can be done without losing much or any of your presumed full head of steam.

A good technique for catamaran jibing was discovered by Keith Notary and Bill Burns of Florida. The crewman simply hangs on to the jib clew, lifts himself from the deck and, with a Tarzan-like scream, swings from one hull to the other (ahead of the mast), directly to his position on the opposite hull. The sail will be drawing all the way through the jibe. It is a little scary at first, but very effective.

Downwind, you may be able to sail far more responsively to wind shifts than you would ever dare going upwind, where each tack costs you so much in forward motion.

How do you recognize headers and lifts downwind? If you and your crew are operating the boat properly (the crew holding the jib steadily so that the helmsman can steer by it down that very thin line between a luff and a stall), then the headers and lifts will be noticed just as quickly as when on the weather leg. You need only read the jib, steer by it, and you can be alert to wind shifts.

For example, if you are steering the boat by the jib downhill and the sails start to luff, you should allow the boat to head a bit deeper. Your heading will be closer to the mark and so you may conclude that you have a header. If, on the other hand, your jib begins to stall and you must head higher to maintain your boat speed and proper jib performance, then your steerage will be farther away from the mark and you are being lifted. But if you are to recognize these shifts the jib must be held steadily in order that you sail by it and sail down that critical thin line between a luff and a stall. Early in your practice of this technique, a compass might be useful, but you should try to develop "feel" for speed and course as soon as possible, as your eyes over the course can produce much richer rewards.

It might be mentioned that some catamarans are by far more critical on the downwind leg than others, and that thin line to which we have been referring becomes very much thinner. After a great deal of practice in a boat that is very critical, imagine jumping into a boat that is not so critical downwind. Chances are you might clean up on that point of sail. To define "critical," think of it as the degree to which the boat sails faster by tacking than by wing and wing. In monohulls, most sailors find it more desirable to sail directly downwind, while some of the gamblers may want to try tacking downwind. The gamblers had better be sailing their boats on a very critical line to beat the running boat, for their increase in boat speed while sailing closer to the wind on a tacking course is not that much greater than that of a straight downwind running boat. It is definitely faster to tack downwind, even in monohulls, but the angle of attack is much more critical on boats that are limited by hull speed.

In the high-performance cats of today you will find that sailing a course closer to the wind makes for a great deal more boat speed than a running course. The increased speed of the tacking course is very significant over the running course. The less that increase in boat speed when on a tacking course, the more critical it is to find the proper angle of attack. A boat with a high-aspect ratio sail plan and slim hulls will no doubt be able to sail much faster by reaching than by running. Its significant increase in boat speed by reaching will make its angle of attack on the downwind course less critical than that of a boat with buoyant hulls and a lower aspect ratio sail, whose boat speed on a reach will increase, but not as much as in the previous design. Even for the second boat it is faster to tack, but to find the angle of attack that is fastest and most efficient will be more difficult, and so it will be a more critical downwind boat.

At first you may find that in your class the running boat is beating you to the leeward pin. If that is true, you simply have not yet found the correct angles. Since the distance is farther on the tacking course, you must be sure that your increase in boat speed not only makes up for the distance, but exceeds it. You must find that perfect angle of attack, that sweet spot, that critical angle where the speed and distance of the tacking boat exceeds the speed and distance of the running boat.

The angle of attack downhill will change in accordance with the conditions of the wind, waves, and weight. In moderate air, in most cats, the angle will be about 45 degrees to the course. It is in this nice, moderate breeze that you should do a lot of practicing to find that sweet spot for downwind tacking. From there you can modify it to meet the condition—light, heavy, whatever. When the air is light and there is no sea to ride out, your angle of attack could be a bit higher to the wind, for you will be trying to keep good boat speed and keep out of stalls. You will find that the boat stalls and dies more easily in lighter air than it does in heavier air. In heavy air you can head much deeper than normal, for you will not only have an apparent wind that is trying to move far forward, but you will more than likely have some nice waves to ride. In heavy air and seas you should head up enough to get good speed, and just as the wave goes under you, head deep quickly, trying to nestle your bow right into the back side of the wave. When you start to overtake the wave, head back up. If you dig into the wave ahead of you, it will slow down your boat and the wave behind—the one you have really been riding—will slip under you and away; you will have lost your free ride. Keep your bow right into the backside of the wave ahead and the one behind will do its job.

If the wind and waves are very awesome, you perhaps could be better off riding wing and wing, or at least an extremely deep tack. Tacking off on a close angle in extreme conditions will do very little good, for you will find a lot of difficulty in handling all the speed and power that you have created by doing so.

We have talked of boat and sail trim and off-the-wind sailing techniques; now let's discuss tactics. If you round the weather mark in the lead of the race or even ahead of someone in particular you wish to beat, you should take the same tack that he does (this is similar to covering as you would do on the weather leg) When he jibes, you should too, for the odds are that if he gets any puffs or shifts, so will you. For example, suppose you are in the lead and go off on starboard from the pin for a hundred yards or so, and your friendly foe the Red Baron rounds the mark and flops to port, and picks up a nice header. You should also go to port, and if you pick up the same header—and you should, since you are staying in the same wind patterns—at that time you will have increased your lead a bit. If the Red Baron jibes to starboard when he gets the next lift, so should you, for you will be possibly throwing him some bad air, and you will still be in the same wind patterns. You will have lost some distance, but you'll be ahead to windward, with your wind shadow effect swinging back at him.

Suppose you had remained on starboard from the mark. You may have picked up a really nice little shift of your own and increased your lead even more, but on the other hand, you could just as easily have gone down the tubes, for it could have been your opponent that got the nice little wind shift. If he does get something good and you are off somewhere else, you're sunk.

When in the lead of a race or near it, you should try to cover the fleet behind you. Should they split, you will have to take a choice of the favorite side of the course, go with the most traffic, go with the opponents that you are most worried about, or possibly split the difference and go up the middle, lightly covering those that seem to be posing the biggest problems. If you go up the middle, you can easily hurry to either side of the course if something major happens over there. Needless to say, if all the boats go on one side—and that rarely happens—cover them. Chances are they will not make it that easy for you, though.

If you are behind, try for clear air and headers all the way down the course, all the time watching those guys ahead to see what they are getting on both sides of the course. Remember to keep the boat going as deep as you can get it to go. Tack to the lifts and hold the headers all the way.

Unlike coming about, jibing is very quick in a catamaran, so do not hesitate to do it. By the way, in jibing, do not put your tiller over too fast, as a superquick turn will slam on the brakes. If you turn too slowly, you will sail into a stall and just bob around until you get headed back up closer to the wind on the opposite tack. The helmsman should warn his crew of the upcoming jibe, then slowly start pulling the helm over, with ever increasing pressure. Then either crew or helmsman should pull the boom through on the way to the other side of the boat. (In light to moderate air the boom-pulling task is necessary, but in heavy air you will not have to worry about it.) The tiller should be constantly tended, for you don't want the boat to straighten out and head downwind while you're scurrying across the deck. Just as in tacking on the weather leg, keep your hold on the tiller all the way through the jibe. As the boom comes across, head the boat back to a reaching direction and resume your "full steam ahead" status.

If, in your travels on the long road of downwind tacking, you find yourself on starboard when you want to be on port, and an opponent is steaming along on port on a collision course, do not exercise your starboard rights. Rather, flop early. The wind shadow on this downwind point of sail is much farther forward than on the weather leg—just about where the monohull shadow is when it is going to weather. So by flopping early you will be able to throw him garbage air and soon leave him even farther behind wallowing in bad air. If he chooses to head up out of your shadow, that creates no problem for you either, for now he is higher (undesirable) and you are lower and out front in clear air. If you had exercised your starboard rights and then jibed, you could easily have found yourself in his wind shadow. All the windward boat has to do is to drive a little deeper on the leeward boat and the leeward boat soon becomes blanketed.

Often in your downwind campaign you will come up on a boat that is below you and ahead. If you are driving your boat deep, as we have been talking about, and still maintaining boat speed, the other boat may be afraid that you will drive over him, and so he will begin to head up higher. Start early and try to get under him far enough in advance not to pick up much of his wind shadow. If you stay high and continue coming up on him, he will try to run you back to the weather mark.

I have repeated my advice to sail as deep as possible a number of times, and I'll repeat it again. Sailing deep has benefits other than getting closer to the mark. Tactically, you have an advantage in sailing deep. Suppose you are the boat slightly ahead and in clear air, and to leeward. The Red Baron drives over you by heading higher and going faster, but you meanwhile keep your cool and head down as deep as possible, still moving well—not as well as Red, but still well. When it comes time to jibe, and you both do so, even without a shift you will find yourself higher than he, but to windward, creating a wind shadow that he must break through. If there had been a lift, you could possibly have lost a little ground to him, but you'd still have him in your wind shadow. If the wind were to head you, you would pull out magnificently ahead of him and could very well lay the mark, while he must jibe twice more. And another thing: You do want to go deep, but not at the sacrifice of speed. You must find that sweet spot of deepness *and* speed. If you do, you have it made, for you will find that 80 percent of your competitors will go too high and the others will go too low.

~11~
Care and Feeding

"You always hurt the one you love . . ." goes the popular refrain, but in the catamaran business it becomes a sort of reverse truism; you are most often hurt by the things you love: sun, water, and speed. The sun that brightens your days also dries out lubricants, robbing rubber, phenolics, and trampolines of their natural oils, and thus their smooth working. The water, particularly the salty variety, eats away at everything and washes away lubricants at the first sign of desiccation. And speed; you will note early in your catamaran experience that lovely humming sound that indicates you are screaming across the water at a very high rate of speed. The hum is vibration, a sneaky devil busy at loosening shackle pins, cross-arm bolts, and rudder pintle mounts, and chewing away at every union of fiberglass and metal.

Knowing you have these fair-weather friends, you will want to arm yourself to cope with them as the price of speed, safety, and the avoidance of economic and personal disaster. The armor you carry need not be extensive. Your shield should be an aerosol can of spray lubricant of the WD-40 type; your lance and spear a screwdriver, pliers (vise grip), and wrenches. Thus armed, you'll find day-to-day racing maintenance a snap.

By the time you have read this far, we must presume you

have long ago learned that the avoidance of a capsize in a cat is dependent on being able to let lines go. The blocks, cam cleats, and other paraphernalia through which these lines pass are generally composed of stainless steel and phenolic or Delrin sheaves and bearings. Doubtless, as a racer, you have bought very good ones and they work dependably while they're new. The secret of keeping them new is a simple can of spray lube. These lubes are colorless, and will not stain even Dacron sails. They have the wonderful side effect of making things look new as well as operate like new. They are harmful to almost nothing on a catamaran, and you should use them liberally and often—like each weekend. Spray each and every block, cam, cleat, roller, rudder pintle, gooseneck part, mast socket, traveler—everything. Every time your mast comes down, spray the sheaves at the head and jib exit, and if you have a halyard lock, spray both sides of that. Most of these products, in the form sold to boaters, come with a tiny detachable tube that allows you to spray this good juice liberally into the bearing systems of your blocks and wherever grease lubrication would be impossible. So get out there and spray!

If you sail in salt water, you must follow the basic one-design practice of hosing down everything with fresh water at the end of each day's sail. As sea water dries out, it leaves a residue of harsh abrasive salt crystals that will attack all the working parts of your boat, including the finish, and remember, your boat works on the trailer on a highway. You may envy that Hobie sailor down the road who just pulls his boat up on the beach and walks away, but ask yourself, if he races, How well does he do? And can *you* afford the 2 or 3 percent efficiency loss that may result from the lack of maintenance?

But where water is concerned, the biggest danger is the

water itself. It weights, it rots, and it is difficult to get rid of in its many forms. Whether you are storing for the winter or for a few hours, try to get your boat as dry as humanly possible. Catamarans are weight-sensitive, and the weight of water is the greatest liability you can carry.

Most modern multihulls are constructed of fiberglass, and no word could ever give more false comfort than "fiberglass." It suggests the water impermeability of a drinking glass. Most fiberglass is laid up with polyester resins as the basic ingredient. Unless your boat is laid with epoxy, that resin acts like a sponge. Don't be deceived by the shiny gel-coat finish that seems to shed water; it can stop the passage of moisture only when it takes on moisture itself. Test data are sketchy, but most lead to the conclusion that a piece of fiberglass immersed in water for only an hour will take on as much as 25 percent of its weight in water. That's a racing handicap you can do without.

Each time you take your boat out of the water, open the drain plugs and follow that up with a sponging out of every trace of water inside. Leave inspection ports open whenever possible, if you have them. Then the sun and wind can turn back into your allies and dry the boat out. With the ports closed, all the sun will do is distribute the trapped moisture throughout the boat, well above the waterline. At home you can speed the process up and make it more thorough by an hour's running of a vacuum-cleaner exhaust through one of the inspection ports. (The exhaust of the cleaner rather than its intake side is recommended, as the exhaust carries with it the warmth of the motor.) But whatever your method, pay attention to moisture if you want to win.

And the problem of speed . . . well, we must trust to your own analytical abilities to tell you what price you are paying for speed on your cat. A Tornado begins to hum at about twelve miles per hour, if it's well tuned; a Hobie 16 at about fourteen. The humming gets louder and more exhilarating as the speed goes up. Think about what causes it: misalignment. Now it is impossible to align all the variables on a catamaran—the true parallel of the hulls, the true parallel of the rudders, the congruence of stream from bow to dagger board to rudder. These little disparities in water flow cause vibration and we hear it as hum. So *daily* check shackle pins, cross-arm bolts, rudder pintle bolts, and key rings. If you don't, they will vibrate loose and cost you a race.

Rudders have been known to fall off if not properly secured to the transom. In most designs the pintles and gudgeons are secured through the transom by a nut and bolt. Check to make sure the nut is tight and that there is a wide, flat washer under it, or it could readily pull through at the wrong time. In the summer of '72 we did a little experimenting with pop rivets to see if they would hold the rudders in place. As I was sailing along in the lead of the last race in the Midwest Championship, one rudder suddenly got wobbly and then fell completely off. I quickly unhooked it and steered the boat with the remaining rudder, but by the next mark that rudder also fell off. So we sailed back into the harbor under sail steering alone, giving up a cinch for a win because we had chosen to use rivets rather than through bolts. It certainly was a lesson. If the cat you have bought has its rudder mounts pop-riveted, drill them out and replace them with stainless bolts.

The rudder head itself has been known to open up. Check carefully for cracks and other signs of strain. They can be repaired by using epoxy glue and stainless bolts and a "Loc-

Tite"-type material. Check the main hinge bolt and make sure it is tight and safetied.

Check the rudder arms, and the various cleats on them. The hiking stick too. In some of the classes an aluminum rod-type hiking stick and tiller bar are used, and though they are light, they do tend to break where they are attached to one another. To correct that, cut the rod at the attaching point, and slip the next size rod over it, sleeve fashion, and then have it secured in place by welding.

The next closest thing to check would be the traveler. If you have a roller-bearing type, be sure to lubricate it well with a good silicone-type lubricant. If you use a pully and cleat stop for the free-wheeling car, be sure they are properly lubricated. Quite often the traveler track will pull out, too. Check to see if the rivets, screws, or bolts are tight or need replacement. Rivets cannot be tightened, so they will have to be drilled and replaced, but that is a quick and easy task. If you have loose screws and they will not tighten, take them out and reinsert them, using epoxy glue to help the adhesion in the screw holes.

All lubes you will use will almost certainly have a petroleum base. These oils have the annoying effect of attracting abrasive dirt and sand. The only answer is a regular cleaning, as demanded by the conditions of sailing and storage. If you sail off a sandy beach, the internal traveler is a menace. It must be rinsed out after each sail, and I find turpentine useful in this connection, after a squirt or two with the hose. If you have no sand problem, once every few months you should wash out all old grease with turpentine (it's oily and will not attack the metal) and replace it with new lube.

Hull maintenance for racing is so controversial, I find myself wishing I could avoid it altogether.

The subject of hull maintenance for racing seems to turn each sailboat owner into an apostle for his own particular method. You probably have already established your own particular preferences by now, and my views will do little to alter them. For the benefit of any readers who are totally new to cat ownership, I'll review some of the most common methods, since obviously it's important to do *something*.

Fiberglass hulls oxidize and dull much like automotive finishes. The waxes in gel coat that give it its new-look shine disappear. At this point the boat is less salable, since most people seem to think that it probably doesn't go through the water as easily as it should. But with all the variables that go into a sailboat's speed measure, there's no proof of that.

For years we used wax—ordinary automotive cleaner-waxes. They kept the hulls shiny and clean and didn't seem to slow us down. Many people still rely on this method, if for no other reason than its simplicity, and there are now a number of special boat waxes that claim to be formulated for boat problems.

Some years ago the process of wet-sanding swept all one-design racing, and a whole cult has grown up around this method, with scientific explanations that would fill a whole chapter. It has one immediate appeal in that it tends to ensure a more fair surface, at the expense of considerable elbow grease. Its adherents argue that the slight roughening of the hulls has the effect of creating a damp layer that presents a water-to-water surface and an ideal effect on the boundary layer created as the boat passes through the water. It doesn't seem to slow anyone down. I do question the general practice of wet-sanding only the area from the waterline down. Small cats sail on a hull that effectively reaches right up to the gunwales, so consider the extent to which you will have to do this armwork before you begin.

In recent years a whole array of specially formulated "go-fast" bottom paints and coatings have appeared and have found both popularity and critics. The first to win favor among catamaran people were the graphite types, a very thick black coating that could itself be sanded, buffed, and polished. Again, these were generally used only from the waterline down. Then there are the colorless wipe-on or aerosol coatings, such as Hydron and Sea Film, which offer one considerable advantage to cat owners: the ease with which they can be used to treat and protect the entire hull and topside. These are formulations of fluorocarbons, Teflon in a polyethylene carrier, and a variety of other magic low-friction words. Measuring improvement in boat speed through a coating on a sailboat is next to impossible under use conditions, but one does have to be somewhat impressed with the figures on reduced fuel consumption in power craft. They do not seem to slow anyone down.

Of the metal parts on your cat, the most frequently in need of review are the shrouds, stays, and trapeze wires. The more you trailer, the more you need to review. Bending and rebending of braided wire cable causes ends to split out from the braid. Downwind, these can rip a sail pressed against them. A bent-over kink will repeat itself until the wire will someday fail in a twenty-five-knotter. There is a very simple, if painful, way to check this. Regularly run your hands up the cables, and when you cut yourself, look for a trouble spot. If as many as *three* strands are broken, replace the whole thing.

Most production cat spars, crossbeams, and other large metal parts are anodized aluminum and don't require care. If yours aren't anodized, clean them up with a good aluminum cleaner and then try one of those fancy "go-fast" hull coatings, sprayed or wiped on. You're in for a surprise. It will save you a whole season of oxidization in the most tropical of our North American settings.

Regularly check diamond stays and their supporting struts and arms. The slot in the spreader arms is usually bushed with plastics, but should it fall out, it can cut through a diamond stay in a day's sail. There is a great deal of load on spreaders and stays, and in this day of slack stays and bending masts, one must be supercautious about any chaffing at the spreader arms. If there is any evidence of chaffing, replace the stays and, if a grommet is not available, file the slot rounded and smooth and wrap it inside and out with a good plastic tape.

How lucky you are to be a cat sailor and be able to roll up your main like a window shade! Catamaran mainsail life (racing, that is) staggers the imagination of a Soling sailor, and the answer is that its full-battened configuration literally dictates proper care. So keep rolling it up, launder it when necessary, take the battens out in the winter—if it will make you feel better. But generally your mainsail will take care of itself.

Not so your jib, however. Watch any average Tornado or Shark fleet start in light air and you will see the damnedest bunch of rags hanging in front of the main. Your jib does an enormous job in that it makes your mainsail efficient. It deserves special care. My own solution to the care problem is a simple transliteration of what we all go through on the main. Fold if you must, but if you want to try something new and exciting, simply roll your jib up along the luff. When you're through, take the big string of spaghetti you've created and coil it and put it in the bag. Any wrinkles created by this technique will not interfere with air flow or trim in light air.

I hope I don't have to remind you that jibs on medium- and small-sized cats are hard to reach and generally go into the water before they come off. Rinse and wash—particularly if you sail in salt water. In addition, this is the sail that slaps about so violently whenever you are in "idle." On a Tornado, Shark, or Hobie 16, this sail is difficult to reach when the boat is in the water, but whenever possible, drop the halyard when you are sitting around or docked waiting for something to happen. The sail will invariably get wet, but it will retain its shape a lot longer. Check the sail constantly for frays, rips, or tears. Whenever you return it to the sailmaker for a repair, ask him to check it to see if it still has the shape and size that it had when he made it. If you want to win, you may find you have to replace a jib even seasonally, whereas a main will last you for many years longer than a racing monohull sail that is not full-battened. If you have a Hobie or Sol Cat with full-battened jib, remember that it still takes the same punishment as any other jib and may lose its shape as fast as a Tornado jib. It just looks better.

Contemporary battens are almost carefree. If you have wooden battens not coated with plastic, you must of course remove them after every sail if there is the slightest bit of moisture—and in salt air, that's every day. Sailmakers now seem to feel that you need not detension battens when storing your sails even for long periods of time. In the old days, we would unlace them if we were putting the boat to bed even for a week. Take your pick of the two philosophies. The one will give you a great deal of spare time, the other will almost force you to think about batten tension in relation to the wind for each series of races.

The slightest rip in a trampoline will undoubtedly cost

you a race if it's not repaired immediately. It's when you're racing that you bounce around most violently and can't take time to care where you step. Tighten the tension on the tramp constantly. Remember that if you can pull up the tramp just one inch, it's that much less hitting the waves in a chop and that much less air resistance. There is nothing aerodynamic about the shape of your rump sticking down below the line of your boat.

Any good racer takes care of his dagger boards (while envying Hobie owners). It is a hateful job, as access or removal is generally tricky. When you first take delivery of a new boat, you will undoubtedly go to work with fine sandpaper and finishing materials. An epoxy paint is my immediate preference, as it will cut down water absorption and its concomitant weight. If you sand thoroughly and cover the entire board, it will never take on a drop until chipped. Finish with wet-sanding or, if you are of that school, a go-fast bottom juice. After every race, check leading edges for chipping or dents, drying out and repairing them as fast as they develop. All of the above for rudder blades, don't forget. On the Tornado and the Shark, the raising and lowering mechanisms on the rudders will have you swearing like a trooper before you own them long. But they must be continually lubricated, fiddled with, and above all checked for any unusual wear or metal "chewing" against wood or metal. Your own racing style may not call for raising and lowering weather rudders, but the first time you get into weeds or kelp during a race, you will be very thankful you have them operable.

Winter storage practices will be in large part dictated by space availability. The ideal is to store the boat on the trailer in a dry building or garage. If you have to demount the boat, the ideal is to hang the hulls, again in a dry place and with free air circulation about them. A spray coating of a WD-40 type of lubricant spray on all metal parts will see them through till spring, when they'll need no more care than wiping off the dust. If you must store outside, don't make a tight tent of plastic over the boat. Moisture will come out of the ground in fall and spring and you will have created a greenhouse better suited to raising geraniums than storing a boat. Protect your boat from rain and snow by laying plastic or canvas over some sort of lath trellis at least a foot above the hulls, extending the same out over the sides, but open on all four sides.

You may be a subscriber to the "wax is bad" philosophy, but there is simply no other way to prevent fiberglass hulls from dulling and from oxidizing the gel coat. So wax for winter storage and re-treat the hulls in the spring.

All this may sound like a hell of a lot of work, but there is a rich reward if you do it and a grim alternative if you don't. Some few years ago, when we were racing wooden-hulled Sharks, maintenance was such a universal problem that few owners really properly kept their boats and hardware up. You just raced the hell out of it and everyone was in the same boat. The Tornado class, where boats are all much newer and where every tiny bit of hardware is so much more critical, is rapidly pointing up the fact that owners who win are the owners whose boats are maintained as fastidiously as a convent kitchen. It's quite a lesson, and I wish I could go back.

~~12~~
Watch It!

Right now I am going to come down hard on you in the tiresome matter of physical condition. Before you decide to skip over this chapter, give me a chance to explain why, in my view, you will have little success at catamaran racing without paying it conscientious attention.

Don't quote me as having said that any gorilla can lumber about a Soling without damaging his racing results seriously. Yet I do believe that among the six Olympic classes, no boat—not even the Finn—is as sensitive and as responsive as the cat to physical and athletic characteristics of their skippers and crews. (There are few better arguments for keeping the Tornado as an Olympic class than that it is a true test of the attributes of an athlete—and that's what the Olympic Games were all about two thousand years ago, and should be about now.) And when I say "athletic," I must quickly point out that I do not refer to strength or size, but to a body well conditioned and coordinated, male or female.

The hottest catamaran racing classes in the world, such boats as the Hobie 16, Tornado, International Class C, Sol Cat, and A-Lion, are almost all marked with fairly fine hulls as opposed to earlier cats, and certainly as opposed to any monohull. Because of their extreme beam, they have an illusionary stability. But don't let the fact that you can step off the dock onto a gunwale delude you. As I have said repeatedly throughout this book, these boats are extremely sensitive to weight, and you can't jump around on a deck or trampoline without hurting your racing chances. The winning skipper and crew will move about the boat swiftly, but with deliberation and coordination. Catamaran rudders look small, but when considered in relation to the speed of the boats and their weight, they are very large. The dagger boards (or the rocker area on Hobies) are a pivot point such as few monohulls can boast, and, again, speed and the extreme linear character of the double hulls can blind you to the very strong forces set up by the rudder.

A jerky, uncoordinated hand on the rudder bar will cost you plenty.

Then there is the inescapable fact that while catamaran sailing can be a gang of fun, it can be a bear. Many is the time that my crew simply refused to participate in that last race, sometimes a bit oblivious of our standings in the series. And there were times I was so worn out that it seemed as if the crew had a good idea. So what?

In the not so good old days of cat racing, when the only active racing classes in North America were the Shark and the P-Cat, and a big fleet was five boats and a big national was twenty, perhaps you could drop a few races. If you didn't beat Tom, Dick, or Harry this week, you could get him back the next, and you could afford to pass up a chance to practice. Not so today. Rarely (assuming you are trying) will you sail a race and not learn something to tuck away in your mental tucker bag, and if you are racing a Hobie, a Tornado, or any class that's big in your area, you will need to have everything tuckable tucked, and not be too tuckered out to tuck away some more in the last race. If you ultimately want to be a winner in catamaran racing, be prepared to practice at every opportunity for good competition. Sail that last race (and be physically fit enough to sail it) whether or not it will have any effect on your last-place (or *first-place*) standing in the series.

To belabor a very important point, during the 1974 season, those of us who sailed in Olympic classes at Olympic training-type regattas were just amazed at the progress of the Canadian sailors since the preceding year. Almost to a man, they credited much of their improvement (particularly in the very athletic Finn class) to the *enforced* physical training program that the Canadian Olympic Committee had made mandatory. If you wanted support for racing in Olympic classes, you had to train with a daily exercise program, often under supervision. It worked.

So now that you agree with me about its importance, how to get there? Whatever physical program you select must be matched to your time, your interests, and what turns you on. But consider what you are after. You want smooth coordination and physical endurance. Weight lifting may allow you to hold your own on Muscle Beach (or heft your Prindle 16 through the surf) but it will be of marginal value for sailing. I try to get my regular exercise by jogging, bicycling, swimming, or simply walking. All these are known contributors to coordinated muscle activity; with the exception of walking, all can contribute to your staying power on the racecourse. If you must compact your exercise periods (and remember: anything daily beats the most arduous weekend program), the famous Royal Canadian Air Force exercises have been published and revised into every conceivable form of program, most taking but eleven minutes each day.

Having dispensed with the notion that raw muscle or brute strength is what we are after, let me restate that all this is a unisex program, and that no girl who goes catamaran racing should consider herself exempt. Presumably the joys of sailing with your husband or buddy have already occurred to you. Let me remind you now that you have more to do each night than put your hair up in curlers. Stay in shape, lovable though that shape may already be.

One of the many husband-wife and girl-and-boy teams I know comes to mind the minute I think of the importance of stamina. I have never seen George and Betsy Alleman leave a series before the last race because they were ahead or because they were behind or because they had third place locked in. Some of us think of George as the Clark Kent of cats, not because of his ability to change clothes in phone booths, but because he is one of the strongest men in sailing. His wife, Betsy, is petite, intensely feminine, and probably far stronger than George for her weight; bright, coordinated, and all the more lovely for that. Both are somewhere in their forties, but it is my bet that it would take quite a team of teenagers to wear them down. If they ever refuse to tack, it isn't because they're worn out.

Now that we have our bodies in shape, let's extend some of that thinking to the boat, with the same coordination, construction, and endurance in mind. When you pick any optional hardware for your cat, you will pick it for lightness—but never so light that it will not stand up under a blow or an emergency, or go to hell the first time you fail to give it some sort of religious maintenance. If you have to worry about a piece of hardware or a fitting on the racecourse, throw it overboard. It's not worth it. It will take your mind off the race and cost you far more than the ounces you save.

I am scarcely the first around to don a life vest, but let me suggest that knowing that they are on board and handy saves another section of my taxed brain—particularly as I often race with my young son as crew. Among the many USCG-approved flotation devices (did you know that if the number on the label has faded, it's not legal?), the most useful for cat racing is the vest type (Elvstrom), as it can be worn without restricting movement.

The next most important item in the peace-of-mind category is a proper anchor and line. If you love your boat and have invested much work in getting it in shape and learning its unique properties, you won't want to see it on the rocks. The anchor should be heavy enough (rated) to hold your boat and it should have its own light line of at least a hundred feet for most offshore waters and deep lakes. On the Tornado, Shark, and other large cats there is ample storage room for this "insurance policy." I appreciate the fact that it can be a liability to stow and weight to carry aboard many boats like the Hobies and smaller cats, but in a severe race offshore in, say, Biscayne Bay, it may keep you and the boat from an unexpected visit to Castro—upside down. Most class racing rules now require that you carry a paddle. If your class does not require it, carry one. There are several new telescopic paddles that fold up into themselves, and some are combination baler pumps. Regardless, a little ingenuity will make even a canoe paddle easily stowed. (Try the Hobie trick of lashing it under the trampoline, where it won't risk fouling a sheet or line.) The first time you are caught in a dead calm, you'll be grateful and will get to the bar before the beer is all gone.

Before you get the idea that I am trying to load you down

with gear in order to beat you (I'm about to bring up pumps, as you suspected), let me tell you a story. I was sailing in a series on Lake Erie in my new fiberglass Tornado. I had not yet discovered that manufacturers can be somewhat careless about affixing rudder hardware with locking washers or resins. It was the last race, and to hold my respectable second place all I needed was a finish. During the race the rudder pintle hardware opened up and the hull flooded. We sank so gradually on one hull that we didn't even notice it until there was considerable water. No sponge! No pump! Tiny little access ports! If we had had a small pump aboard . . . Enough said?

For the next peace-of-mind item, let's go back to the field of athletics and ask ourselves why every other type of athlete warms up, from track stars to skiers, yet we see sailor after sailor going out to freeze. It doesn't make sense.

Sail warm!

Your body will work better and more smoothly if it isn't chilled. And you know perfectly well that air over water is considerably colder than air over land, and carries a greater chill factor. Some of the country's most chilling sailing weather is found year-round in San Francisco. Local cat sailor Joe Siudzinski makes some very practical suggestions:

When sailing on the Bay, you *are* going to get wet! Opinions vary, but the consensus suggests the following: a turtleneck shirt, possibly covered by a sailing vest, and a light-colored (bright orange is best) nylon jacket with hood over the whole works; swim trunks under the (optional) wet-suit-type booties inside the oversize deck shoes being almost a "must." The turtleneck shirt keeps the wet suit from cutting the neck, and a towel around the neck keeps that cold water from dripping down. Standard foul-weather gear is also used by some of our best crews, but must provide a snagfree environment for the wearer. Being cold, wet, and miserable is not conducive to pleasure sailing!

Amen. So, starting with Mr. Siudzinski's stern formula, take it off in progressively warmer conditions—but better warm than cold. In the Can-Am Championships at Hamilton, Ontario, the whole country was under clouds and rain, except there in Hamilton—the home of Ken Robertson, the living legend of multihullers. The Hamilton Chamber of Commerce ordered up sunny skies and beautiful temperatures. Out I went in my bathing suit, soon to discover that the temperatures on that lake were unbelievably low. As the spray flew and the wind increased, the chattering of my teeth seemed to be causing the fiberglass hulls to hum. Between races I did a quick change into more sensible clothing and picked up three places in the next race.

Now, to complete the peace-of-mind notes, let me make a strong suggestion that you take a tip from our friends who fly planes and set up for yourself a preflight checklist. Go over this list before each day's sailing (a lot can happen overnight in a two-day regatta).

This will have to be called a prelaunch checklist, for heading the list before you head for any hoist or water should be: "Close drain plugs." These are the easiest thing to forget on a cat, and the penalties are infinitely more severe than on a monohull. My cousin John Tuel and I were readying ourselves for the fourth race of the Tornado Worlds in Florida and did a fine job of preparing and drying out the boat. Since we were early, we launched ahead of the rush and tied her up at a nearby mooring and went to relax under a palm and discuss a few tactics. One by one all of the boats filed out of the harbor and it was time to cast off. Much to our chagrin, we had forgotten to close a drain hole, and she was sinking. Scratch the first race and sail the rest of the day with a soggy, slushy hull.

Second on a checklist (and very important for two- and three-day events) is to check the rigging to make absolutely sure that every shackle (particularly all the stainless types, for they work loose with alarming frequency) is firmly closed. Check the rigging for frays, burs, or slack. A boat sitting overnight on the beach and being flayed by strong winds can change dramatically from the sound ship you left yesterday.

Have you a tool kit on board? It need not be a big one, but it is worthless left on the beach or incomplete because you raided it to make a repair. And it must contain vise-grip pliers. This is the do-all tool, and with one aboard you can feel you are in safe jaws. They can release shackles under pressure, tighten nuts of any size, cut rigging, untie hardbound knots, cut line, talk to you when you're lonesome, and perform such minor surgery as removing slivers. Once the lock on the winch drum broke and down came the main. But, thanks to the vise-grip, up it went again, and by locking the tool on the winch drum and up against the mast, I got it to stay there under proper tension.

Perhaps the only other tool you need in your sailing kit (assuming you have done your preparation well) is a good rigging knife, *sharp*! If you feel you will ruin it by using it as a small screwdriver, add one of those. Add to your checklist a bowline so that you don't have to strip your anchor or mainsheet should you have to be towed or take refuge at a strange dock. I hope it goes without saying that all this will be stowed where you and your crew know where it is, and *off the deck*! (And we don't mean tucked under the hiking strap, where the first big wave will carry it away.)

Add to your personal checklist any tuning refinements you may be in the habit of using, and finish it off with the admonition to check all running rigging to see that it is not fouled before casting off. In cats, the sails can do more of the steering than the tiller. So if you suddenly find the jib sheet fouled in a crowded mooring area, you may be on the way to buying a piece of a Columbia 50—or knocking an honest competitor out of the day's racing. We know one sailor who overlooked the fact that his mainsheet flogged around and tied itself into a knot. The minute he cast off, he was over with a mooring can stuck through his mainsail.

With the checklist concept, you can use your mind on the racecourse for the business at hand—good racing!

—13—
Whoops!

No doubt about it: everyone, even an ardent multihuller like myself, would rather right a Laser than a Hobie 14. Certainly I would prefer righting a 470 to a Tornado. It becomes pretty obvious that the "Ease of Righting" Trophy must go to the monohull, while the "Hard to Capsize" Trophy belongs to cats. Trimarans deserve an extra medal.

Still, cats do capsize. Prevention is certainly the best cure for all multihulls. Though they are easier to right, the owner of the beach boat variety, such as Hobie, Cal Cat, Sea Spray, and that sort, should also pay heed.

In very heavy air or puffy air, I believe it is insane to cleat a main, or to have so many purchases on the mainsheet that you cannot release it quickly. In puffs you should be able to respond immediately to the variable winds and release the main. In extremes, the jib could receive the same treatment.

The modern ratchet block has been a big help along the lines of safe sheet handling. If things are properly set up, one should be able to hold the main in a close-hauled position with very little effort, yet be able to release quickly. My present setup is such that the pressure on a heavy day can be held with two fingers, yet when release is necessary, the

A good way to look pretty and a bad way to sail a cat—too much heel and the draft in the main is way aft of the 50% area.

sheet rolls out freely. With this efficient rigging you can play the puffs and ease the main in and out to keep the windward hull just skimming the water, and not scarily always nearing calamity.

Sailing to weather in racing conditions, you will probably try to ride out the occasional strong gust by feathering to weather with the helm. Sometimes a puff will slam you a good clout, putting you 'way up in the air. Here you should quickly let out the mainsheet, but not to the point where you slam the hull back down hard. As the windward hull reaches its peak in altitude and you have eased the main, she will start down pretty fast. If it has not started down and is hanging there, ease the main more, for you are subjecting yourself to a possible capsize. One more fresh puff and over you'd go. As the hull starts down, harden up the main fast; you will not only stop the boat from slapping the water hard, but also put on a sudden burst of speed. It's sort of like squeezing a grape. This technique will take considerable practice for many, both to overcome excessive fear and to get a feel for realistic limits. But the rewards are enormous.

Sometimes the jib should be released too. If your main is out as far as it will go and you are still hanging there, for the sake of aridity, let the jib out. If you don't, you may very likely go swimming instead of sailing.

At Lake Canandaigua, New York, at a Nationals, the wind was howling down off the surrounding mountains and into the narrow valley lake. The wind was very shifty and gusty. It would head you . . . and head you . . . and head you—all the time you were heading down with the wind shift to keep your boat moving—then *wham!* A terrific blast would catch you from abeam and up the hull would fly. What a thrill! In that case, my crew had the jib cleated, but always ready for an instant release. It was released, too, quite a few times.

So far we have been discussing anticapsize techniques for upwind and close reaching. Tacking downwind requires a different approach. Tacking very deep, you may still be able to keep your crew on the leeward hull, hand-holding the jib, even in some fairly stiff weather. Regardless, the jib should never be cleated downwind in the rough stuff. Again, the main is not cleated, and you should have a ready hand on the traveler release.

When that blast of wind hits you now, you do not head up to windward as you did when close-hauled, but rather you drive off deeper downwind. You and your crew may have to shift your weight 'way aft, particularly on boats without reserve buoyancy forward, such as the Hobie. Going farther downwind will lower the lifting hull, and your only concern now is not to bury the bows.

In these downwind circumstances it appears that various boats have various tendencies. The Tornado has little plane deck area with its sleek bow entry, and while it slices deep into the water, it seldom seems to trip into a pitchpole. The Shark has never been known to pitchpole, owing to its tremendous buoyancy in the bow. The new Sizzler appears to be one of the first of the small cats that does not tend to trip on her leeward bow. The Australis and Unicorn have bow entries similar to that of the Tornado and seem docile enough. While the Hobies are not given to dangerous and violent pitchpoling, they will capsize bow first when overpowered—but slowly.

At any rate, when all the sails are out all the way, and you are still in trouble, do not panic and head up, but rather make sure you keep it going deep. Be careful not to steer so deep that you near the point of sailing by the lee, or an accidental jibe. The boat should settle down and the bows should come rising out of the water like a German U-boat in the North Sea and you will swiftly skim along downwind until the blast gets by.

If the blast is somewhat lighter and is simply lifting you slightly, do not worry too much, but tend the helm. Often the sail can overpower the rudders. I have seen the time when the wind was so strong that we simply held the jib enough to catch a few feet of its leech, helping the steering, let the main out, and sailed on just that amount of power. We made better and safer time than our comrades, who were swimming around waiting for the crash boat.

As a generality, organization is most important in the prevention of overturning. A clean deck is a must: Anything cluttering up your decks can easily foul the sheet at the wrong time. Clear, crisp commands usually help, for in the rage of the sea, words can be muddled and are quite often confused, if heard at all.

The crew can be a big help by watching for sheets that have washed out of the boat and are dragging in the water behind. A beginning sailor would probably think that there is really nothing too seriously wrong with dragging sheets, except that you might unexpectedly snag a pompano or king mackerel, but he would be quite wrong. For example, if the mainsheet comes directly from the last block to the skipper's hand and then trails back into the water, he will not be able to release the mainsheet when a puff comes. As he tries to ease the sheet through his hand, it will go nowhere, for the drag of the water coupled with the resistance of the line trying to run through the skipper's hand holds it from running freely. The crew should definitely keep those sheets inside the boat.

Sheets do get outside the boat easily, for as the water rushes over the leeward hull, a lot of splash comes into the main cockpit, and it all has to run out. Out with the water run the sheets.

There are principally three situations in which most capsizes occur. The beam and broad reach is the primary one, which we have just covered. The second most important is the jibe, and third, coming about. In monohulls you will find the order reversed, with jibing first and coming about second; reaching or just sailing is 'way down the line. The biggest spiller in monohulls is the "chute."

Jibing can be a real art. Let us speak first of the preparation for a jibe, for the crew must be alerted that there is going to be a change in setting. The typical barks of "Ready about" and "Hard alee" serve very nicely and give the crew a chance to get organized.

On your command "Hard alee," don't expect the command to be taken too literally. At first ease the tiller across, and when at the dead downhill position, when the sail is about to flop, go ahead and hit it hard, but be prepared to head it back downwind again in a hurry. When the sail flops over, the power of it will automatically want to steer the boat back upwind; that is why you must be prepared to steer back downwind—to counteract the mainsail force.

It is very easy to get disorganized as to where the mark is—and where you are, for that matter—when jibing. But start by looking immediately at telltales or whatever you choose by which to steer downwind, establishing immediate orientation. The more quickly you get organized, the less your chance of overturning.

If you find that after the jibe you are beginning to raise a hull, head it back downwind quickly. The main should be all the way out, too. Once you are off on your new tack, then trim to whatever you desire, meanwhile keeping the sails slack. This temporary reorganization should not hurt your overall boat speed, unless you spend an undue amount of time figuring out what is going on.

The traveler can be a problem for some boats, depending on the rigging used. I have my boat rigged with a roller-bearing traveler. A line comes from the traveler through a cleat block in dead center and into the cockpit. It's long enough to reach from the traveler car to the center of the rear beam (when it is set at its farthest outboard position), and then from there it should be long enough to reach approximately halfway up the length of the cockpit. Thus I can reach it from almost anyplace I am sitting. The virtue of this rig is seen in reaching and jibing. In reaching, you can keep your main flat, and by easing the traveler, adjust the trim. But the true virtue is in the jibe. You can set the traveler car sheet at the far outboard position, and when you jibe, the traveler car will run freely to the other side and stop at exactly the same spot. With the hand friction or double cleat setup that many use, the skipper has to pull the traveler all the way to center before every jibe.

Any sailor brought up in the monohull school knows that when jibing a monohull, you must sheet in all the way through the jibe, so that the boom doesn't slap over and knock you down, but not so in the catamaran. The cat's speed is nearing that of the wind itself and the boom slapping over is not dangerous. (You still want to be ready to head it back down, as previously mentioned.) The monohull is limited to hull speed, and if the wind is exceeding the hull speed by much, the slapping over of the main could well be its demise.

Usually I preset my traveler to a position about a foot short of the outboard gunwale, merely to save damage to the traveler. When the boom slaps over, the pressure is then put on the whole traveler track, not just the end section of it. If that slap were to pull on just the end of the track, it might well pull the track out by the screws, rivets, or whatevers.

Centerboards can be a help or a hindrance in your jibe. While centerboards make steering easier and more responsive, they also allow the boat more easily to fly hulls, because of increased lateral resistance underwater. There are definitely two schools of thought on them.

One sailor may prefer to reduce wetted surface by pulling his boards up and then struggle a little more with the tiller in puff, trying to hold the boat on its course downwind. If the boat is not well balanced, that struggle might well be lost, for in puffs the terrific concentration of wind on the main wants to round the boat up to windward—and could possibly do it; and here is our hero (with less wetted surface) struggling to hold the boat's heading downwind. Two things may be happening: First, the struggling is caused by the rudders' attempts to overcome the steering power of the main; second, those rudders, fighting the water, are now acting as brakes. What was gained in speed by less wetted surface is lost by increased drag.

The real virtue of this sailor's idea is that he has very little chance of capsizing, for indeed the boat will not tip very easily with no boards. He may rip off his rudders and end up floundering helplessly, and then capsize for lack of steerage.

The next sailor prefers both boards down, affording him ease of steering. Yet in a jibe or a big puff he runs an even greater risk of capsizing. However, he will be able to steer himself out of trouble better than the first sailor.

The third sailor takes the middle road, and probably the best one. He sails the broad reach with his windward board down, getting the best of both worlds. His windward centerboard gives him good steerage with less resistance, he has reduced wetted surface somewhat, and he is less subjected to capsize, for the leeward hull, without a board, is not likely to cause hull flying.

Upon command to jibe, he raises his windward board, comes about, and when reaching the windward side of the boat, lowers the board. All through the jibe he is boardless and not quite so subject to capsize, while after he regains his organization he has the best of both worlds again.

In the art of tacking when going into the wind, there is very little that is dangerous, other than the fact that you must get to the windward side posthaste.

As in jibing, clear, crisp commands are necessary, and organization is essential. If the tacking is not done properly, you will be certain to get yourself in irons. Any one or a combination of things can get you into irons. Irons are pretty dangerous in a monohull, but less so in a multihull. It is simply disturbing to watch your competitors fly by at a maddening pace. But hold on and you'll be out of irons in a moment.

You are now head to wind and either stopped dead or beginning to drift backward. Assume you wish to flop to starboard. Have your crew quickly backwind the jib on the starboard side. You should then push your tiller so as to turn the rudders to starboard, and if the situation warrants it, push the main out on the port side of the boat. You will be backing up and then suddenly, with all these reverse pressures going on, the stern will push off to starboard and your bows will fall off to port. At that point, have the jib snap through and be hardened up on the port side. Leave the main alone until the boat begins to move, then pull in the main and start steering.

~~14~~
Bottoms Up

If you were not paying much attention in the last chapter and took it all with a grain of salt, then you may very well be sitting quietly on your hulls (upside down by now), listening to your crew cuss you out at 140 words per minute (wpm), with gusts of 180. Do not let that bother you, though, O fearless tar; just toss the poor devil a bar of Lifebuoy while we analyze what we could have done.

As the hulls began to rise, you should have uncleated the mainsheet and been easing it out. If that's not the entire answer, the jib would have been next. Meanwhile, you and your crew should have been hiking out as far as possible. With all that done, however, the boat is still rising, and now you are in trouble and you know you are going over.

Frame that picture! From here you can save the puppy from turning turtle. You and your crew should both be crawling back over the hull toward the centerboard from your hiking position. One of you—preferably that agile deck ape—should swing down quickly to the lower centerboard and get out on it as far as possible. The other mate should quickly do the same on the upper centerboard. In most catamarans this will effect a balanced teeter-totter, with the gunwales being the fulcrum. The wind force that was strong enough to knock

All sheets released. Your weight should bring the boat back down, but strong winds under the hulls may continue to push you over without help from your sails.

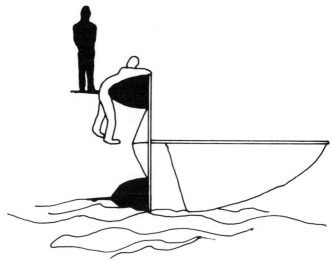

Immediately—and we mean immediately—your crew should be out of the trapeze and out on the centerboard as far as he can get. Skipper should slide down to lower hull as quickly as possible as his weight up there will turn boat into turtle position.

Skipper stands on lower centerboard and can help by pulling on dolphin striker or better yet a righting line. It's a waiting game now til the wind turns the boat into the wind.

Now, with the wind blowing onto the decks, the mainsail should come up out of the water and you will come back to upright quite quickly once the wind gets under the sail. Crew can scamper aboard as the boat comes over, but the skipper is in for a bath. He deserves it in all probability.

you down will now be strong enough to be a big help in getting you back up. Just sit tight there on the centerboards, doing your little balancing act, and let the wind blow the boat around like a weather vane, mast pointing into the wind. Now that wide multihull, complete with trampoline, will form a huge barn-door effect. The same wind that had blown over your sail now has a chance to blow over the barn door, and in doing so to raise the mast. Once the mast rises about a foot off the water, the wind additionally catches the sail and up she'll come.

When I first got into catamarans, my instructor was the famous George Alleman. George casually explained to me that should I go over, I should quickly swim to the end of the mast to keep it from turning turtle. If I could not swim that fast, I should run out on the sail, but in any case, get to the end of the mast and hold that end from going under. After accomplishing that masterful feat, George said, I should begin working my way toward the boat and pushing up on the mast all the way at the same time, and before you could say "Jack Robinson" the boat would pop up.

I had filed this information away in my tiny brain, and even found myself allowing it to escape from my lips while trying to advise other new cat sailors on how to save themselves from a fate worse than death. One such sailor was my brother Bill. Bill was not too crazy about sailing in the first place, but he decided to go along.

On this one particular bright, sunny day, Bill decided to borrow my boat. The wind was blowing about fifteen knots, and since he was a novice, he was concerned about what to do in case of a capsize. I casually explained to him the procedures he should use, describing all he had to do and how to do it.

Sure enough, the gusts started coming and Wee Willie capsized. He plunged into the water, quickly swam to the end of the mast, and held the end up. Much to Bill's surprise, in holding the end of the mast up out of the water, he held himself well underwater. So Bill would hold the mast up for a minute, then come up for a gasp of air; then back under for a minute, then back up for air. The poor chap kept this procedure up doggedly and kept making repeated bubbling attempts at saying "Jack Robinson."

Later we pulled the beautiful cat off the rocks, totally smashed. As the Coast Guard arrived, Bill calmly stood there and said, "Now I suppose you're going to give me a parking ticket!" Bill gave up sailing on that day and took up scuba diving.

We have come a long way since then. The correct way to save a boat was discovered by Mike Rubin and Bob Fortune at a race in Vermilion, Ohio. Lake Erie had really kicked up on a very blustery day and these two discovered the technique of getting out on the centerboards, and then passed it on to me.

A year later I had my chance to try out the technique as my son and I were sailing a series race at Sandusky, Ohio, and a squall line hit us. We capsized quickly, but were still near our hiking positions. My son decided to plunge headlong into the water and head for the mast, while I decided to try the Rubin-Fortune method. With the extremely strong winds in the storm, the boat quickly drifted away from my son, and there I was all by myself, sitting out on the centerboard on the upper hull. I started scooting out toward the end of the board and watched the mast rise from about four feet below the surface. It rose slowly, but as the wind weather-vaned, the boat around it began to rise more quickly, and before long it was only a foot below the surface. I scooted out a little farther on the board and then started hiking, praying that the board would not break. The mast slowly came out of the water. The wind caught under the sail and up she came. I jumped aboard and went back after my son. So righting a boat and saving it from turtle can even be done single-handed.

Things must be done with dispatch so that you can immediately balance the boat on the fulcrum point—the gunwale. Since you are hiking, it is a simple matter of slipping right on over back onto the boards. The important thing for the racing skipper to learn quickly is not, under any circumstances, to get caught unawares and slide downhill to the leeward hull. This will speed up your capsize and greatly increase the chances of turtling.

It has previously been mentioned that the same wind that knocked you down will right you, and I offer as evidence an incident that occurred at a big national regatta that I had helped host. The races were blessed with a lot of air, and for a novelty we decided to schedule a demonstration on how to execute the Rubin-Fortune method of righting a boat. The commodore's nickel that had brought air for the regatta ran short because of inflation, and the air began dropping drastically for the demonstration. To get the beast of a boat over, my crew trapezed and I hiked out the leeward side. It finally went over and there it stayed. That was when we discovered that if you don't have enough wind to get it over, you don't have enough wind to get it back up. It was quite embarrassing when the crowd of spectators ashore broke out in laughter; and I ate crow.

Beach boats such as the Hobie Cats, Prindles, and so on, which have no centerboards, luckily sport fairly deep rockers that provide the same platform for righting. In addition, their smaller size enables them to be righted—even from a turtled position—without outside assistance. You and your crew stand on one hull and pull on the crossbar, dolphin striker, or, better yet, a righting rope. When the mast comes parallel with the water, the rest of the procedure is the same.

Suppose you are not quick enough and you let your Tornado, Shark, or other large cat turn over to the dreaded turtle position. Luckily, someone happened upon a way to right the turtled catamaran without tearing up the sails, breaking battens, or stretching rigging.

First off, don't panic when the boat gets turtled, for the upside-down catamaran is very, very stable. In fact, the inverted position should allow you a lot of time to get out some 600 grit wet-and-dry sandpaper and clean up some of those nicks on the bottom. A nice lawn chair would also make the wait for help a little more comfortable. But don't leave the boat. Remember, the boat in this position is very safe.

While you're waiting for help, get a line tied around the base of the mast. When help arrives, have your rescuer take your line that is tied to the mast and pull straight off your stern, as if to tow the boat backward. You and your crew should sit on the stern, forcing it underwater. The power-boat should pull quite steadily and with ever increasing power. As the powerboat pulls and you hold down the stern, the transoms and trampoline will become a huge scoop and sea brake, while the bow will become light. As the bows rise higher out of the water, the speed of the pulling boat should increase and the cat should come upright very easily, end over end.

There should be practically no damage to sails or rigging with this technique. The sails will be coming out of the water with little or no resistance, just like the huge dorsal fins of sailfish. Since there is very little resistance in pulling cats up this way, it has been done with the pulling boat being another sailboat.

Back in the olden days they tied a line on the chain-plate area of one hull and ran a line across the two hulls and on to a powercraft. When the powerboat began to pull, however, the boat would not stay perpendicular, nor would the line stay straight across it, probably owing to a tremendous amount of resisting forces underwater. I have witnessed this type of rescue, and it took two strong men to hold the line and boat in place while the powerboat struggled away. With all the resistance underwater, an awful lot of things have to stretch and give, and generally break.

The modern method is the only way to right a turtled catamaran of the large type. (1) Tie a line to the mast base and run it along the bottom side of the boat and aft to the pulling boat. (2) Crewmen should get to the sterns of the boat and force them under, forming a water scoop. (3) The powerboat should apply steady, ever increasing power from the sterns of the turtled boat, until righted end over end.

Index

A-Lion, 117
Alleman, Betty, 120
Alleman, George, 7, 41, 42, 120, 138
Alter, Hobie, 3
Aquacat, 63
Australis, 10, 129

Backing up, 67, 68
Backwinding, 71
Barber hauler, 34, 35
Battens, 39-43
  bolts, 13
  mainsail, 12
  material, 40, 41, 42
  measurement, 12
  stiffness, 12, 39, 40, 82, 83
  wear, 19, 113
  weight, 12, 39, 40
Burns, Bill, 99

Cal Cat, 56
Capsize, 126, 142
Carpenter, Dr. Jack, 8, 15
Catamaran
  backing up, 67, 68
  history, 2

Centerboards, 94, 95
  care, 115, 133
Chop, 52, 54, 58, 83, 84
Class C Catamaran, 117
Coatings, bottom, 112
Crew duties, 85, 86, 96, 98, 99, 130, 135
Crew weight placement, 45-50
Cunningham, 13, 14
Curtaindale, Bill, 61

Downwind sailing, 51-60

Fiberglass, 41
  care, 113, 114
Footing, 82, 84
Fortune, Bob, 139, 140

Garner, Dr. Parrish, 56

Heard, Gayle, 3
Heavy air sailing, 59
Helmsmanship, 61-65, 92
Herold, Larry, 85
Hobbyhorsing, 58, 83

Hobie Cats
  14, 16, burying bow, 129
  14, 16, righting, 140, 141
  16, jib, 29
  14, steering, 65
  16, weight balance, 55
  weight placement, 60

Irons, avoidance, 69

Jellison, Bill, 68
Jib, 29-39
  battens, 29
  care, 113, 114
  leads, 30, 31, 32
  luff control, 36, 37, 38
  shape, 32, 33
  traveler, 33, 34, 35
  use going to weather, 79, 80

Kettenhoffen, Bob, 3

LeCain, Jim, 7
Leech lines, 18, 20, 21, 22
Leeway, 84

MacAlpine-Downey, Rod, 3
Mainsail, 5-28
  traveler adjustment, 82, 95, 110,
    131, 132
  twist, 83
Maintenance, 106-116
Marsh, Rodney, 3
Mast
  bending, 13
  rotation, 15, 16, 17, 18, 20
McIlvray, Dick, Jr., 5, 14
Melges, Buddy, 64

Notary, Keith, 99

P-Cat-Pacific Catamaran, 46
Phoenix, 47
Pinching, 84, 85, 90
Port tack start, 75, 76
Prindle 16, 140
Pyle, Carter, 3, 56

Racing starts, 66-77
Reaching, 91-105
Righting, 140, 141, 142
Robertson, Ken, 123
Rubin, Mike, 139, 140
Rudder drag, 51, 94
Running, 91-105

Saltwater, special problems, 107
Schuh, Jack, 8
Seaman battens, 42
Seaman, Gary, 42
Shape, sail
  mainsail, 10-17
Shark Catamaran, 16, 33, 46, 59
Shearwater Catamaran, 46
Siudzinski, Joe, 122, 123
Sol Cat, 10
Spreader, 16
Stan, Nick, 7
Starting lines, 74, 75
Starting races, 66-77
Stays, diamond, 15, 113
Steering, 61-65
Stoppers, mast rotation, 15

Tacking
  downwind, 98, 99
  when to, 87, 88, 89
Tactics, 86, 87, 88, 93, 102, 103,
  104, 105
Taylor, Rick, 3
Telltales, 97
Tornado
  mainsail, 9

performance, 3
  weight placement, 47
Trampoline maintenance, 114, 115
Trapeze, 49, 50
Tuel, John, 123
Turtle position, 141, 142

Unicorn, 10, 129
  weight balance, 55

Weather, boat, 78
Weather sailing, 78-90
Weight, placement, 45-50, 54
Wells, Betty, 6
Wells, Bill, 6
White, Dave, 62
White, Reg, 3, 7
Windshift, 89
Woodruff, Stan, 20